Effective C++

Addison-Wesley Professional Computing Series

Brian W. Kernighan, Consulting Editor

Ken Arnold/John Peyton, *A C User's Guide to ANSI C*

Tom Cargill, *C++ Programming Style*

David Curry, *UNIX System Security: A Guide for Users and System Administrators*

Robert B. Murray, *C++ Strategies and Tactics*

Scott Meyers, *Effective C++: 50 Specific Ways to Improve Your Programs and Designs*

Radia Perlman, *Interconnections: Bridges and Routers*

David Piscitello/A. Lyman Chapin, *Open Systems Networking*

Stephen A. Rago, *UNIX System V Networking*

W. Richard Stevens, *Advanced Programming in the UNIX Environment*

Effective C++

50 Specific Ways to Improve Your Programs and Designs

Scott Meyers

ADDISON-WESLEY PUBLISHING COMPANY

Reading, Massachusetts   Menlo Park, California   New York
Don Mills, Ontario   Wokingham, England   Amsterdam
Bonn   Sydney   Singapore   Tokyo   Madrid   San Juan   Paris
Seoul   Milan   Mexico City   Taipei

Many of the designations used by manufacturers and sellers to distinguish their products are claimed as trademarks. Where those designations appear in this book and Addison-Wesley was aware of a trademark claim, the designations have been printed in initial capital letters.

The programs and applications presented in this book have been included for their instructional value. They have been tested with care, but are not guaranteed for any particular purpose. The publisher does not offer any warrantees or representations, nor does it accept any liabilities with respect to the programs or applications.

The publisher offers discounts on this book when ordered in quantity for special sales.
For more information please contact:

> Corporate & Professional Publishing Group
> Addison-Wesley Publishing Company
> One Jacob Way
> Reading, Massachusetts 01867

Cover design by Joyce Weston
Front cover photo by Hank DeLespinasse, The Image Bank
Back cover photo of the author by Nancy L. Urbano
Text set in ITC Bookman (text) and Courier (code samples) by the author using FrameMaker software on a SPARCstation I workstation. Camera-ready copy was produced from Adobe Postscript on a Scitex Dolev/PS.

ISBN 0-201-56364-9

Text printed on recycled and acid-free paper.
5 6 7 8 9 10 11 12 MU 96959493
Fifth printing, July 1993

For Nancy,
without whom nothing
would be much worth doing.

Wisdom and beauty form a very rare combination.

– Petronius Arbiter
Satyricon, XCIV

Contents

Classes and Functions: Design and Declaration   60

Classes and Functions: Implementation   96

Preface

This book is a direct outgrowth of my experiences teaching C++ to professional programmers through the Institute for Advanced Professional Studies. I found that most students, after a week of intensive instruction, felt comfortable with the basic constructs of the language, but were less sanguine about their ability to put the constructs together in an effective manner. Thus began my attempt to formulate short, specific, easy-to-remember guidelines for effective software development in C++: a summary of the things that experienced C++ programmers either almost always do or almost always avoid.

As a computer scientist, I was originally interested in rules that could be checked by a machine. To that end, I outlined a program to examine C++ software for constructs that were "almost always wrong." Currently under development, this checking program has become known as lint++. However, it quickly became apparent that the great majority of the guidelines used by good C++ programmers were too difficult to formalize, or had too many important exceptions, to be blindly enforced by a lint++-like program.

That led me to the notion of something less precise than a computer program but still more focused and to-the-point than a general C++ textbook. The result you now hold in your hands: a book containing 50 specific suggestions on how to improve your C++ programs and designs.

In this book you'll find advice on what you should do, and why, and what you should not do, and why not. Fundamentally, of course, the whys are much more important than the whats, but from a purely pragmatic point of view, it is much more convenient to have a list of guidelines in front of you than it is to memorize a textbook or two.

Unlike most books on C++, my presentation here is not organized around particular language features. That is, I don't talk about constructors in one place, about virtual functions in another, about inheritance in a third, etc. Instead, each explanation is tightly coupled to the specific guideline it accompanies, and my coverage of the various aspects of a particular feature is typically dispersed throughout the book.

The advantage of this approach is that it better reflects the complexity of the software systems for which C++ is often chosen, systems in which the understanding of individual language features is not enough. For example, experienced C++ developers know that understanding inline functions and understanding virtual destructors does *not* necessarily mean that you understand inline virtual destructors. Such battle-scarred developers recognize that comprehending the *interactions* between the features in C++ is of the greatest possible importance in using the language effectively. The organization of this book reflects that fundamental truth.

The disadvantage of my approach is that you may have to look in more than one place to discover everything I have to say about a particular construct in C++. To minimize the inconvenience inherent in this approach, I have sprinkled cross-references liberally throughout the text, and a comprehensive index is provided at the end of the book.

The set of guidelines in this book is far from exhaustive, but coming up with good rules — ones that are applicable to almost all applications almost all the time — is harder than it looks. Perhaps you know of additional guidelines, of more ways in which to program effectively in C++. If so, I would be delighted to hear about them.

On the other hand, you may feel that some of the items in this book are inappropriate as general advice; that there is a better way to accomplish a task examined in the book; or that one or more of the technical discussions is unclear, incomplete, or misleading. I encourage you to let me know about these things, too.

Donald Knuth has a long history of offering a small reward for people who notify him of errors in his books. The quest for a perfect book is laudable in any case, but in view of the number of bug-ridden C++ books that have been rushed to market, I feel especially strongly compelled to follow Knuth's example. Therefore, for each error in this book that is reported to me — be it technical, grammatical, typographical, or otherwise — I will, in future printings, gladly acknowledge the first person to report that error.

Send your suggested guidelines, your comments, your criticisms, and
— sigh — your bug reports to:

Scott Meyers
c/o Editor-in-Chief, Corporate and Professional Publishing
Addison-Wesley Publishing Company
1 Jacob Way
Reading, MA 01867
U. S. A.

SCOTT DOUGLAS MEYERS   PROVIDENCE, RHODE ISLAND
                                                     NOVEMBER 1991

Acknowledgments

Almost exactly twenty years ago, Kathy Reed taught me what a computer was and how to program one. In the two decades that have passed since then, I've moved from a 110-baud teletype to a 12-MIPS workstation, and from BASIC to C++, but through it all, the excitement she engendered in me has remained.

In 1989, Donald French asked me to develop C++ training materials for the Institute for Advanced Professional Studies, and since that time he has given me the opportunity to use, refine, and extend those materials. Had he not done so, I wouldn't know C++ well enough to discuss it in public, much less write a book about it. When I did decide to write this book, Don provided more than just moral support, he also introduced me to John Wait at Addison-Wesley, an act of incalculable value and one for which I am deeply grateful.

The students in the class at Stratus Computer during the week of June 3, 1991, were not the first ones to suggest that I write a book summarizing the pearls of alleged wisdom that tumble forth when I teach, but they were the ones who finally convinced me to do it. I started writing this book the day after the course ended. I am indebted to them for pushing me over the edge.

In general, the items and examples in this book have no particular source, at least not one that I can remember. Rather, they grew out of a combination of my own experiences using and teaching C++, those of my colleagues, and opinions expressed by contributors to the Usenet newsgroups `comp.lang.c++` and `comp.std.c++`. Many examples that are now standard in the C++ teaching community — notably strings and complex numbers — can be traced back to the first edition of Bjarne Stroustrup's *The C++ Programming Language* (Addison-Wesley, 1986); many of the items found here (e.g., Item 17) can also be found in that seminal work. Item 9 was motivated by commentary in *The Annotated C++ Reference Manual* (see Item 50), and Items 10 and 13 were suggested by John Shewchuk. Doug Lea provided the aliasing examples at the end of Item 17, and Mark Linton set me straight in my thinking about grasshoppers and crickets in Item 43. Of course, "Hello world" comes from *The C Programming Language* by Brian W. Kernighan and Dennis M. Ritchie (Prentice-Hall, 1978). Alexander Wolf and Stan Lippman provided valuable last-minute help with templates.

The implementation of `operator new` in Item 10 is based on one presented in the second edition of Stroustrup's *The C++ Programming Language* (Addison-Wesley, 1991).

Partial and/or complete drafts of the manuscript were reviewed by Tom Cargill, Glenn Carroll, Tony Davis, Brian Kernighan, Jak Kirman, Doug Lea, Moises Lejter, Eugene Santos, Jr., John Shewchuk, John Stasko, Bjarne Stroustrup, Barbara Tilly and Nancy L. Urbano. Their comments and suggestions on technical, expository, and grammatical issues greatly improved the book you now hold.

I am greatly indebted to the following people, each of whom brought to my attention one or more errors or other shortcomings in previous printings of this book; I have listed these alert readers in the order in which I received their reports: Nancy L. Urbano, Chris Treichel, David Corbin, Paul Gibson, Steve Vinoski, Tom Cargill, Neil Rhodes, David Bern, Russ Williams, Robert Brazile, Doug Morgan, Uwe Steinmueller, Mark Somer, Doug Moore, David Smallberg, Seth Meltzer, Oleg Shteynbuk, David M. Papurt, Tony Hansen, Peter McCluskey, Stefan Kuhlins, David Braunegg, Paul S. R. Chisholm, Adam Zell, Mike Kaelbling, Natraj Kini, Lars Nyman, and Greg Lutz. Needless to say, I alone bear responsibility for the errors that inevitably remain.

John Wait, my editor at Addison-Wesley, has been a delight to work with from start to finish. Both entertaining and informative, he has been helpful in more ways than I could imagine, and on a fair number of topics that I didn't even know existed.

Finally, I must gratefully acknowledge the enthusiastic and unflagging encouragement provided to me by my wife, Nancy L. Urbano, and by my family and hers. In spite of the fact that writing a book on C++ was the last thing I was supposed to be doing, and that it reduced my free time from merely little to effectively none, they made it unmistakably clear that the effort was worth it if, in the end, the result was an author in the family.

Introduction

Learning the fundamentals of a programming language is one thing; learning how to design and write *effective* programs in that language is something else entirely. This is especially true of C++, a language that boasts an uncommon range of power and expressiveness. Built atop a full-featured conventional language (C), it also offers a wide range of object-oriented features. Support for templates (parameterized types) has recently become available, and constructs for handling exceptions are in the language specification (though not yet in most commercial compilers).

Properly used, C++ can be a joy to work with. An enormous variety of software designs, both object-oriented and conventional, can be expressed directly and implemented efficiently. You can define new data types that are all but indistinguishable from their built-in counterparts, yet are substantially more flexible. A judiciously chosen and carefully crafted set of classes — one that automatically handles memory management, aliasing, initialization and clean-up, type conversions, and all the other conundrums that are the bane of programmers the world over — can make application programming easy, intuitive, efficient, and nearly error-free. In short, it isn't unduly difficult to write effective C++ programs, *if* you know how to do it.

Used without discipline, C++ can lead to code that is incomprehensible, unmaintainable, inextensible, inefficient, and just plain wrong.

The trick, then, is to discover those aspects of C++ that are likely to trip you up, and to learn how to avoid them. That is the purpose of this book. I assume that you already know C++ as a *language* and that you have some experience in its use. What I provide here is a guide to using the language *effectively*, so that your software is efficient, maintainable, extensible, and likely to behave as you expect.

The advice I proffer falls into two broad categories: general design strategies, and the nuts and bolts of specific language features.

The design discussions concentrate on how to choose between different approaches to accomplishing something in C++. How do you choose between inheritance and templates? Between templates and generic pointers? Between public and private inheritance? Between private inheritance and layering? Between function overloading and parameter defaulting? Between virtual and nonvirtual functions? Between pass-by-value and pass-by-reference? It is important to get these decisions right at the outset, because an incorrect choice may not become apparent until much later in the development process, at which point its rectification is often difficult, time-consuming, demoralizing, and expensive.

Even when you know exactly what you want to do, getting things just right can be tricky. What's the proper return type for the assignment operator? How should `operator new` behave when it can't find enough memory? When should a destructor be virtual? How do you implement a class constant? How should you write a member initialization list? It's crucial to sweat details like these, because failure to do so almost always leads to unexpected, possibly mystifying, program behavior. More importantly, the aberrant behavior may not be immediately apparent, giving rise to the specter of code that passes through quality control while still harboring a variety of insidious undetected bugs, ticking time-bombs just waiting to go off.

This is not a book that must be read from cover to cover to make any sense. You need not even read it from front to back. The material is broken down into 50 items, each of which stands more or less on its own. Frequently, however, one item will refer to others, so one way to read the book is to start with a particular item of interest and then follow the references to see where they lead you.

The items are grouped into general topic areas, so if you are interested in discussions related to a particular issue, such as memory management or object-oriented design, you can start with the relevant section and then either read straight through or start jumping around from there. You will find, however, that all the material in this book is pretty fundamental to effective C++ programming, so almost everything is eventually related to everything else in one way or another.

This is not a reference book for C++, nor is it a way for you to learn the language from scratch. For example, I'm eager to tell you all about the gotchas in writing your own `operator new` (see Items 7, 8, and 9), but I assume that you can go elsewhere to discover that that function must return a `void*` and that its first argument must be of type `size_t`. There are a number of good introductory books on C++ that contain information such as that.

The purpose of *this* book is to highlight those aspects of C++ programming that are usually treated superficially or ignored entirely. Other books describe for you the different parts of the language; this book tells you how to combine those parts so that you end up with effective programs. Other books tell you how to get your programs to compile; this book tells you how to avoid problems the compiler won't tell you about.

Like most languages, C++ has a rich folklore that is usually passed down from programmer to programmer as part of the language's grand oral tradition. This book is my attempt to record some of that accumulated wisdom in a more accessible form.

At the same time, this book limits itself to legitimate, *portable*, C++. Only language features that are in the ANSI draft standard (as expressed in *The Annotated C++ Reference Manual* — the "ARM" — see Item 50) have been used here. Sometimes that can seem restrictive. For example, Item 32 examines the problem of implementing class-specific constants that are available at compile-time. One popular compiler allows you to do it like this:

```
// an unportable way to implement class constants
class X {
private:
  const BUFFER_SIZE = 1024;      // intended class constant

  int buffer[BUFFER_SIZE];

  ...

};
```

Simple and straightforward though this is, it's not allowed by the proposed ANSI standard, so Item 32 suggests a different mechanism for accomplishing the same thing, a mechanism that *is* supported by the proposed standard. In this book, portability is a key concern, so if you're looking for implementation-dependent hacks and kludges, this is not the place to find them.

Unfortunately, it is a simple fact of life that C++ as described by the ARM is sometimes quite different from the C++ made available to you by your friendly neighborhood compiler vendor. In particular, nested types, templates, and exception handling (see Item 49) are all in the ARM, but as I write this in the autumn of 1991, there's not a single publicly-available compiler that supports all three of these features, and there are few that support even two of them.

As a result, when I point out situations in which these features will be particularly useful, I also show you how to get on with the very real problem of producing effective software in their absence. After all, it would be foolish to labor in ignorance of what the future is sure to bring, but by the same token, you can't just put your life on hold until the latest, greatest, be-all-and-end-all C++ compiler magically appears on your computer. You've got to work with the tools available to you, and this book helps you do just that.

One thing you *will not* find in this book is the C++ Gospel, the One True Path to perfect C++ software. Each of the 50 items in this book provides guidance on how to come up with better designs, how to avoid common problems, how to achieve greater efficiency, but none of the items is universally applicable. Software design and implementation is a complex task, one that is invariably colored by the constraints of the hardware, the operating system, and the application, so the best I can do here is to provide *guidelines* for achieving better programs.

If you follow all the guidelines all the time, you are unlikely to fall into the most common traps surrounding C++, but by their very nature guidelines have exceptions. That's why each item has an explanation. The explanations are the most important part of the book, because only by understanding the rationale behind an item can you reasonably determine whether it applies to the program you are developing and to the unique constraints under which you toil.

The best use of this book, then, is to gain insight into how C++ behaves, why it behaves that way, and how to use its behavior to your advantage. Blind application of the items in this book is clearly inappropriate, but at the same time, you probably shouldn't violate any of the guidelines without having a good reason for doing so.

There's no point in getting hung up on terminology in a book like this; that form of sport is best left to language lawyers. However, there is a small C++ vocabulary that everybody should understand. The following six terms crop up often enough that it is worth making sure we agree on what they mean.

For the purposes of this book, a *declaration* tells the compiler about the name of an object or function without providing any details. These are declarations:

```
extern int x;                      // object declaration
void makeUpperCase(char *s);       // function declaration
```

A *definition*, on the other hand, provides the compiler with the details. For objects, the definition is where the compiler allocates memory for the object. For functions, the definition provides the code body:

```
int x;                             // object definition
```

```
    void makeUpperCase(char *s)     // function definition
    {
      unsigned length = strlen(s);
      for (unsigned i = 0; i < length; i++)
        s[i] = toupper(s[i]);
    }
```

That brings us to constructors. A *default constructor* is one that can be called without any arguments. Such a constructor either has no parameters at all or has a default value for every parameter. You need a default constructor if you want to define arrays of objects:

```
    class A {
    public:
      A();                          // default constructor
    };
    A arrayA[10];                   // 10 constructors called

    class B {
    public:
      B(int x = 0);                 // default constructor
    };
    B arrayB[10];                   // 10 constructors called,
                                    // each with an arg of 0

    class C {
    public:
      C(int x);                     // not a default constructor
    };
    C arrayC[10];                   // error!
```

You may find that your compiler rejects arrays of objects when the class's default constructor has default parameter values. For example, many compilers would choke on the definition of arrayB above, even though it receives the blessing of the ARM. This is an example of the kind of discrepancy that can exist between the ARM's description of C++ and a particular compiler's implementation of the language. Every compiler I know has a few of these kinds of shortcomings. Until compiler vendors catch up to the (still evolving) standard, be prepared to be flexible, and take solace in the certainty that someday in the not-too-distant future, the C++ described in the ARM will be the same as the language accepted by C++ compilers.

Incidentally, if you want to create an array of objects for which there is no default constructor, the usual ploy is to define an array of *pointers* instead. Then you can initialize each of the pointers separately by calling new:

```
    C *ptrArray[10];                // no constructors called
```

```
ptrArray[0] = new C(22);        // allocate and construct
                                // 1 C object
ptrArray[1] = new C(4);         // ditto

...
```

Back on the terminology front, a *copy constructor* is used to initialize
an object with a different object of the same type:

```
class String {
private:
  char *data;

public:
  String(const char *value = 0);
                                // default constructor

  String(const String& x);      // copy constructor
};

String s1;                      // call default constructor
String s2(s1);                  // call copy constructor
String s3 = s2;                 // call copy constructor
```

Probably the most important use of a copy constructor is to define
what it means to pass and return objects by value. As an example,
consider the following (inefficient) way of writing a function to concat-
enate two String objects:

```
String operator+(String s1, String s2)
{
  String temp;

  delete [] temp.data;
  temp.data =
    new char[strlen(s1.data) + strlen(s2.data) + 1];
  strcpy(temp.data, s1.data);
  strcat(temp.data, s2.data);

  return temp;
}

String a("Hello");
String b(" world");
String c = a + b;               // c = String("Hello world")
```

This operator+ takes two String objects as parameters and returns
one String object as a result. Both the parameters and the result will
be passed by value, so there will be one copy constructor called to initialize s1 with a, one to initialize s2 with b, and one to initialize c with
temp. In fact, there might even be some additional calls to the copy
constructor if the compiler decides to generate intermediate temporary
objects, which it is allowed to do. The important point here is that
pass-by-value *means* "call the copy constructor."

By the way, you wouldn't actually write operator+ for Strings like this. Returning a new String object is correct (see Item 23), but you would want to pass in the two parameters by reference (see Item 22).

The next two terms we need to grapple with are *initialization* and *assignment*. An object's initialization is when it is given a value for the very first time. For objects of classes or structs with constructors, initialization will *always* be accomplished by calling a constructor. This is quite different from object assignment, which is when an object that is already initialized is given a new value.

```
String s1;                        // initialization
String s2("Hello");               // initialization
String s3 = s2;                   // initialization

s1 = s3;                          // assignment
```

From a purely operational point of view, the difference between initialization and assignment is that the former is performed by a constructor while the latter is performed by operator=. In other words, the two processes correspond to two completely different function calls.

The reason for the distinction is that the two kinds of functions must worry about different things. Constructors usually have to check their arguments for validity, whereas most assignment operators can take it for granted that their argument is legitimate (because it has already been constructed). On the other hand, the target of an assignment, unlike an object undergoing construction, may already have resources allocated to it, and these resources typically must be released before the new resources can be assigned. Frequently, one of these resources is memory, and before an assignment operator can allocate memory for a new value, it must first deallocate the memory that was allocated for the old value.

Here is how a String constructor and assignment operator might be implemented:

```
// a possible String constructor
String::String(const char *value)
{
  if (value) {                    // if value ptr isn't null
    data = new char[strlen(value) + 1];
    strcpy(data,value);
  }
  else {                          // handle null value ptr
    data = new char[1];
    *data = '\0';                 // add trailing null char
  }
}
```

```
// a possible String assignment operator
String& String::operator=(const String& rhs)
{
  if (this == &rhs)
    return *this;                    // see Item 17

  delete [] data;                    // delete old memory
  data =                             // allocate new memory
    new char[strlen(rhs.data) + 1];
  strcpy(data, rhs.data);

  return *this;                      // see Item 15
}
```

Notice how the constructor must check its parameter for validity, and how it must take pains to ensure that the member data is properly initialized, i.e., points to a char* that is properly null-terminated. On the other hand, the assignment operator takes it for granted that its parameter is legitimate. Instead, it concentrates on detecting pathological conditions, such as assignment to itself (see Item 17), and on deallocating old memory before allocating new memory. The differences between these two functions typify the differences between object initialization and object assignment. By the way, if the "[]" notation in the call to delete is new to you (pardon the pun), Item 5 should dispel all your confusion.

One additional term that warrants discussion is *client*. A client is a programmer, one who uses the code you write. When I talk about clients in this book, I am referring to people looking at your code, trying to figure out what it does; to people reading your class declarations, attempting to determine whether they want to inherit from your classes; to people examining your design decisions, hoping to glean insight into their rationale.

You may not be used to thinking about your clients, but I'll spend a good deal of time trying to convince you to make their lives as easy and straightforward as you possibly can. After all, you yourself are a client of the software that other people develop, and wouldn't you want them to make things easy and straightforward for you? Besides, someday you may find yourself in the uncomfortable position of having to use your *own* code, in which case your client will be you!

In the code examples in this book, I have tried to select meaningful names for objects, classes, functions, etc. Many books, when choosing identifiers, embrace the time-honored adage that brevity is the soul of wit, but I'm not as interested in being witty as I am in being clear. I have therefore striven to break with the tradition of using cryptic identifiers in books on programming languages. Nonetheless, I have at times succumbed to the temptation to use two of my favorite parameter names, and their meanings may not be immediately apparent, especially if you've never done time on a compiler-writing chain gang.

The names are `lhs` and `rhs`, and they stand for "left-hand side" and "right-hand side," respectively. I use them as parameter names for functions implementing binary operators, especially `operator=` and arithmetic operators like `operator+`. For example, if a and b are objects representing complex numbers, and if complex numbers can be added via a global `operator+` function, then the expression

```
a + b
```

is equivalent to the function call

```
operator+(a, b)
```

and, as you will discover in Item 23, I declare `operator+` like this:

```
Complex operator+(const Complex& lhs, const Complex& rhs);
```

As you can see, the left-hand operand, a, is known as `lhs` inside the function, and the right-hand operand is known as `rhs`.

I've also chosen to abbreviate names for pointers according to this rule: a pointer to an object of type `T` is often called `pt`, "pointer to T." Here are some examples:

```
class String;
String *ps;                    // ps = ptr to String

class Airplane;
Airplane *pa;                  // pa = ptr to Airplane

class BankAccount;
BankAccount *pba;              // pba = ptr to BankAccount
```

I use a similar convention for references. That is, `rs` might be a reference-to-`String` and `ra` a reference-to-`Airplane`.

Finally, I occasionally use the name `mf` when I'm talking about member functions.

On the off chance there might be some confusion, any time I mention the C programming language in this book, I mean the ANSI-sanctified version of C, not the older, less strongly-typed, "classic" C.

Shifting from C to C++

Getting used to C++ takes a little while for everyone, but for grizzled C programmers, the process can be especially unnerving. Because C is effectively a subset of C++, all the old C tricks continue to work, but many of them are no longer appropriate. To C++ programmers, for example, a pointer to a pointer looks a little funny. Why, we wonder, wasn't a reference to a pointer used instead?

C is a simple language. All it really offers is macros, pointers, structs, and functions. No matter what the problem is, the solution will always boil down to macros, pointers, structs, and functions. Not so in C++. The macros, pointers, structs, and functions are still there, of course, but so are private and protected members, function overloading, default parameters, constructors and destructors, user-defined operators, inline functions, references, and more. The design space is much richer in C++ than it is in C: there are just a lot more options to consider.

When faced with such a variety of choices, many C programmers hunker down and hold tight to what they're used to. For the most part, that's no great sin, but some of those old C habits run contrary to the spirit of C++. Those are the ones that have simply *got* to go.

1   Use `const` and `inline` instead of `#define`.

This item should really be called, "prefer the compiler to the preprocessor," because `#define` is not part of the language *per se*. That's one of the problems. When you do something like this,

```
#define ASPECT_RATIO 1.653
```

the symbolic name ASPECT_RATIO is never seen by the compiler; it's removed by the preprocessor before the source code ever gets to the compiler. As a result, the name ASPECT_RATIO doesn't get entered into the symbol table. This can be confusing if you get an error during compilation involving the use of the constant, because the error message will refer to 1.653, not ASPECT_RATIO. If ASPECT_RATIO was defined in a header file you didn't write, you'd have no idea where that 1.653 came from, and you'd probably waste a lot of valuable time tracking it down. This problem can also crop up in a symbolic debugger, because, again, the name you're programming with isn't in the symbol table.

The solution to this sorry scenario is simple and succinct. Instead of using a preprocessor macro, define a constant:

```
const float ASPECT_RATIO = 1.653;
```

This approach works like a charm. There are two special cases worth mentioning, however.

First, it's sometimes convenient to define class-specific constants, and that calls for a slightly different tack; Item 32 describes what you have to do in that case. Second, things can get a little bit tricky when defining constant pointers. Because constant definitions are typically put in header files (where many different source files will include them), it's important that the *pointer* be declared const, usually in addition to what the pointer points to. To define a constant string in a header file, for example, you have to write const *twice*:

```
const char * const authorName = "Scott Meyers";
```

For a distressingly complete discussion of the meanings and uses of const, including these, see Item 21.

Getting back to the preprocessor, another common (mis)use of the #define directive is to implement macros that look like functions but that don't actually incur the overhead of a function call. The canonical example is computing the maximum of two values:

```
#define MAX(a,b)  ((a) > (b) ? (a) : (b))
```

This little number has so many drawbacks, it's painful just to think about them. You're better off playing in the freeway during rush hour.

Whenever you write a macro like this, you have to remember to parenthesize all your arguments when you write the macro body; otherwise you can run into trouble when somebody calls the macro with an expression. But even if you get that right, look at all the weird things that can happen:

```
int a = 1, b = 0;

MAX(a++, b);            // a is incremented twice
MAX(a++, b+10);         // a is incremented once
MAX(a, "Hello");        // comparing ints and ptrs
```

Here you have a situation in which what happens to a inside MAX depends on what a is being compared with, plus you have lost all vestiges of type safety. In fairness, the last call will elicit a warning from many compilers, but of course the warning message says nothing about MAX, because MAX doesn't exist as far as compilers are concerned.

Fortunately, you don't need to put up with this kind of nonsense. You can get all the efficiency of a macro plus all the predictable behavior and type-safety of a regular function by using an inline function (see Item 33):

```
inline int MAX(int a, int b) { return a > b ? a : b; }
```

Now this isn't quite the same as the macro above, because this version of MAX can only be called with ints, but templates (see Item 49) fix that problem quite nicely:

```
template<class T>
inline T& MAX(T& a, T& b)
{ return a > b ? a : b; }
```

This template generates a whole family of functions, each of which takes two objects of the same type and returns a reference to the greater of the two objects. Because you don't know what the type T will be, you pass and return by reference for efficiency (see Item 22).

You say your compiler doesn't support templates yet? Don't despair. In that case, you can use the preprocessor (of all things) to generate the appropriate inline functions:

```
#define GENERATE_MAX(T)                    \
inline T& MAX(T& a, T& b)                   \
{ return a > b ? a : b; }

GENERATE_MAX(int);              // generate MAX for ints
GENERATE_MAX(double);           // generate MAX for doubles
GENERATE_MAX(String);           // generate MAX for Strings
```

This last example should reassure you that there is still a need for the preprocessor in C++ programs, it's just that it's used differently. Though #define is no longer needed for constants and inline functions, it may be used in other ways, and there is still a need for #ifdef and #ifndef, etc., for controlling conditional compilation.

2   Prefer `iostream.h` to `stdio.h`.

Yes, they're portable, yes, they're efficient, yes, you already know how to use them, yes, yes, yes, but venerated though they are, the fact of the matter is that scanf and printf and all their ilk could use some improvement. In particular, they're not type-safe and they're not extensible. Because type safety and extensibility are cornerstones of the C++ way of life, you might just as well resign yourself to them right now.

Besides, the `printf`/`scanf` family of functions separate the variables to be read or written from the formatting information that controls the reads and writes, just like FORTRAN. It's time to bid the 1950s a fond farewell.

Unsurprisingly, these weaknesses of `printf`/`scanf` are the strengths of `operator>>` and `operator<<`.

```
int i;
ComplexInt c;                    // c is a complex integer

cin >> i >> c;
cout << i << c;
```

If this code is to compile, there must be functions `operator>>` and `operator<<` that take an object of type `ComplexInt`, period. If these functions are missing, it's an error. (The versions for `int`s are standard.) Furthermore, the compiler takes care of figuring out which versions of the operators to call for different variables, so you needn't worry about specifying that the first object to be read or written is an `int` and the second is a `ComplexInt`.

In addition, objects to be read are passed using the same syntactic form as are those to be written, so you don't have to remember silly rules like you do for `scanf`, where if you don't already have a pointer, you have to be sure to take an address, but if you've already got a pointer, you have to be sure *not* to take an address. Let the C++ compiler take care of all those details; it has nothing better to do, and you *do* have better things to do. Finally, note that built-in types like `int` are read and written in the same manner as are user-defined types like `ComplexInt`; try *that* using `scanf` and `printf`.

Here's how you might write an output routine for a class representing complex integers:

```
class ComplexInt {
private:
  int r, i;                    // real, imaginary parts
                               // of number
public:
  ComplexInt(int realPart = 0, int imagPart = 0);

  ...

  friend ostream& operator<<(ostream& s, const ComplexInt& c);
};
```

```
// output value (x, y) as "x+yi" or "x-yi"
ostream& operator<<(ostream& s, const ComplexInt& c)
{
  s << c.r;                  // output real part
  if (c.i >= 0)
    s << '+';                // output sign, if necessary
  s << c.i << 'i';           // output imaginary part, then 'i'

  return s;
}
```

The output format generated by this particular version of operator<< for ComplexInt objects could be refined in several ways, but it's a reasonable first cut at the job. In addition, it demonstrates some fairly subtle, but still crucially important points that are discussed elsewhere in this book. For example, operator<< is a global friend function, not a member function (Item 19 explains why), and the ComplexInt object to be output is passed into operator<< as a reference-to-const rather than as an object (see Item 22).

The corresponding input function, operator>>, would be declared and implemented in a similar manner.

Reluctant though I am to admit it, there are some situations in which it may make sense to fall back on the tried and true. First, most current implementations of iostream operations are less efficient than the corresponding C stream operations, so it's possible (though unlikely) that you may have an application in which this makes a significant difference. Bear in mind, though, that that says nothing about iostreams *in general*, only about particular implementations. Second, there isn't yet such a thing as an official "standard" iostream library (but the ANSI committee for C++ is working on one), so applications that must be maximally portable might want to shy away from the less commonly used portions of the iostream libraries that are currently available. Finally, because the classes of the iostream library have constructors, and the functions in <stdio.h> do not, there are rare occasions involving the initialization order of global objects (see Item 47) where the standard C library may be more useful simply because you know that you can always call it with impunity.

Even though there is no official standard for the iostream library, you can rely on the existence of operator>> and operator<<, and the following classes are almost certain to exist in the eventual standard:

```
istream, ostream, iostream      // basic I/O functionality

ifstream, ofstream, fstream     // file I/O

istrstream, ostrstream,         // array-like I/O (replaces
strstream                       // sprintf and sscanf)
```

(For a detailed description of the proposed iostream library standard, consult a comprehensive, *recent*, introductory textbook such as the second edition of Stanley B. Lippman's *C++ Primer* (Addison-Wesley, 1991), the second edition of Bjarne Stroustrup's *The C++ Programming Language* (Addison-Wesley, 1991), or Arthur E. Anderson's and William J. Heinze's *C++ Programming and Fundamental Concepts* (Prentice Hall, 1992). Because iostreams are part of a library and are not in the C++ language proper, you can't get information on them from the ARM (see Item 50).)

The type-safety and extensibility offered by the classes and functions in the iostream library is more useful than you might initially imagine, so don't throw it all away just because you're used to <stdio.h>. After all, even after the transition, you'll still have your memories.

3   Use new and delete instead of malloc and free.

The problem with malloc and free (and their variants) is simple: they don't know anything about constructors and destructors.

Consider the following two ways to get space for an array of String objects, one using malloc, the other using new:

```
class String {
public:
  String(const char *value = 0);
  ~String();
};
String *stringArray1 =
  (String *) malloc(10 * sizeof(String));
String *stringArray2 = new String[10];
```

Here stringArray1 points to enough memory for 10 String objects, but no objects have been constructed in that memory. Furthermore, without using the placement syntax for new (see Item 8), you have no way to initialize the objects in the array. In other words, string-Array1 is pretty useless. In contrast, stringArray2 points to an array of 10 fully constructed String objects, each of which can safely be used in any operation taking a String.

Nonetheless, let's suppose that you magically managed to initialize the objects in the stringArray1 array. Later on in your program, then, you'd expect to do this:

```
free(stringArray1);
delete [] stringArray2;
```

The call to free will release the memory pointed to by stringArray1, but no destructors will be called on the String objects in that memory. If the String objects themselves allocated memory, as String objects are wont to do, then all the memory they allocated has been lost. On the other hand, when `delete` is called on `stringArray2`, a destructor is called for each object in the array before any memory is released.

Because `new` and `delete` interact properly with constructors and destructors, they are clearly the superior choice.

Combining `new` and `delete` in the same program with `malloc` and `free` is a bad idea. It is undefined what happens when you try to call `free` on a pointer that you got from `new`, or `delete` on a pointer that you got from `malloc`. This can lead to some interesting complications. For example, the `strdup` function commonly found in `<string.h>` takes a string and returns a copy of it:

```
char * strdup(char *p);         // return a copy of what
                                // p points to
```

At many sites, both C and C++ use the same version of `strdup`, so the memory allocated inside the function comes from `malloc`. As a result, unwitting C++ programmers calling `strdup` might overlook the fact that they must use `free` on the pointer returned from `strdup`. But wait! To forestall such complications, some sites might decide to rewrite `strdup` for C++ and have this rewritten version call `new` inside the function, mandating that callers later use `delete`. As you can imagine, this can lead to some pretty nightmarish portability problems as code is shuttled back and forth between sites with different forms of `strdup`.

Given that `malloc` and `free` are ignorant of constructors and destructors, and given that a combination of `malloc`/`free` with `new`/`delete` can be more volatile than a fraternity rush party, you're just *asking* for trouble if you do anything but stick to an exclusive diet of `new`s and `delete`s.

4   Prefer C++-style comments.

The good old C comment form works in C++ too, but the newfangled C++ comment-to-end-of-line form has some distinct advantages. For example, consider this situation:

```
if ( a > b ) {
  // int temp = a;          // swap a and b
  // a = b;
  // b = temp;
}
```

Here you have a code block that has been commented out for some reason or other, but in a stunning display of software engineering, the programmer who originally wrote the code actually included a comment to indicate what was going on. When the C++ comment form was used to comment out the block, the embedded comment was of no concern, but there could have been a serious problem had everybody chosen to use C-style comments:

```
if ( a > b ) {
  /*  int temp = a;                  /* swap a and b */
       a = b;
       b = temp;
  */
}
```

Notice how the embedded comment inadvertently puts a premature end to the comment that is supposed to comment out the code block.

C-style comments still have their place. For example, they're invaluable in header files that will be processed by both C and C++ compilers. Still, if you can use C++-style comments, you are often better off doing so.

It's worth pointing out that retrograde preprocessors that were written only for C don't know how to cope with C++-style comments, so things like the following sometimes don't work as expected:

```
#define LIGHT_SPEED 3e8          // m/sec (in a vacuum)
```

Given a preprocessor unfamiliar with C++, the comment at the end of the line becomes *part of the macro!* On the other hand, as is discussed in Item 1, you shouldn't be using the preprocessor to define constants anyway.

Memory Management

Memory management concerns in C++ fall into two general camps: getting it right and making it perform efficiently. Good programmers understand that these concerns should be addressed in that order, because a program that is dazzlingly fast and astoundingly small is of little use if it doesn't behave the way it's supposed to. For the most part, getting things right means calling memory allocation and deallocation routines correctly. Making things perform efficiently, on the other hand, often means writing custom versions of the allocation and deallocation routines themselves.

On the correctness front, C++ inherits from C one of its biggest headaches, that of potential memory leaks. In C, a memory leak arises whenever memory allocated through `malloc` is never returned through `free`. Even virtual memory, wonderful invention though it is, is finite, and not everybody has virtual memory in the first place. The names of the players in C++ are `new` and `delete`, but the story is much the same. On one hand, the situation is improved somewhat by the presence of destructors, because they provide a convenient repository for calls to `delete` that all objects must make when they are destroyed. On the other hand, there is more to worry about, because calls to `new` implicitly call constructors and calls to `delete` implicitly call destructors. In addition, there is the complication that you can define your own versions of `new` and `delete`, both on a global and a per-class basis, and this gives rise to all kinds of opportunities to make mistakes. The following items should help you avoid some of the most common ones.

5 Use the same form in corresponding calls to `new` and `delete`.

What's wrong with this picture?

```
class String {
public:
  String(const char *value = 0);
  ~String();
};

String *stringArray = new String[100];

...

delete stringArray;
```

Everything here appears to be in order — the call to new is matched with a call to delete — but something is still very much amiss: your program's behavior is undefined. At the very least, 99 of the 100 String objects pointed to by stringArray are unlikely to be properly destroyed, because their destructors will probably never be called.

When you call new, two things happen. First, memory is allocated, and second, one or more constructors are called for that memory. When you call delete, two other things happen: one or more destructors are called for the memory, then the memory is deallocated. The big question for delete is this: how many objects are residing in the memory being deleted? The answer to that determines how many destructors have to be called.

Actually, the question is simpler: does the pointer being deleted point to a single object or to an array of objects? The only way for delete to know is for you to tell it. If you don't use brackets in your call to delete, delete assumes that a single object is pointed to. Otherwise it assumes that an array is pointed to.

```
String *stringPtr1 = new String;

String *stringPtr2 = new String[100];

...

delete stringPtr1;            // delete an object

delete [] stringPtr2;         // delete an array of
                              // objects
```

What would happen if you used the "[]" form on stringPtr1? The result is undefined — meaning don't even *think* about doing it if you want to have a reliable program. What would happen if you didn't use the "[]" form on stringPtr2? Well, that's undefined too.

The rule, then, is simple: if you use [] when you call new, you must use [] when you call delete. If you don't use [] when you call new, don't use [] when you call delete.

This is a particularly important rule to bear in mind when you are writing a class containing a pointer data member and also offering multiple constructors, because then you've got to be careful to use the *same form* of new in all the constructors to initialize the pointer member. If you don't, how will you know what form of delete to use in your destructor? For a further examination of this issue, see Item 11.

6 Call delete on pointer members in destructors.

Most of the time, classes performing dynamic memory allocation will call new in the constructor(s) to allocate the memory, and will later call delete in the destructor to free up the allocated memory. This isn't too difficult to get right when you first write the class, provided of course that you remember to call delete on *all* the members that could have been assigned memory in *any* constructor.

However, the situation becomes more difficult as classes are maintained and enhanced, because the programmers making the modifications to the class may not be the ones who wrote the class in the first place. Under those conditions, it's easy to forget that adding a pointer member almost always requires each of the following:

- Initialization of the pointer in each of the constructors. If no memory is to be allocated to the pointer in a particular constructor, it should be initialized to 0.

- Deletion of the existing memory and assignment of new memory in the assignment operator. (See also Item 17.)

- Deletion of the memory in the destructor.

If you forget to initialize a pointer in a constructor, or if you forget to handle it inside the assignment operator, the problem usually becomes apparent fairly quickly, so in practice those issues don't tend to plague you. Failing to delete the pointer in the destructor, however, often exhibits no obvious external symptoms. Instead, it manifests itself as a subtle memory leak, a slowly growing cancer that will eventually devour your address space and drive your program to an early demise. Because this particular problem doesn't usually call attention to itself, it's most important that you keep it in mind whenever you add a pointer member to a class.

Note, by the way, that deleting a null pointer (i.e., one with value 0) is always safe (it does nothing). Thus, if you write your constructors, your assignment operators, and your other member functions such that each pointer member of the class is always either pointing to valid memory or is null, you can merrily delete away in the destructor without regard for whether you ever actually called new for the pointer in question.

Needless to say, there's no reason to get fascist about this item. For example, you certainly don't want to call delete on a pointer that was never initialized with a call to new, and you almost *never* want to delete a pointer that was passed to you in the first place. In other words, your class destructor usually shouldn't be calling delete unless your class members were the ones who called new in the first place.

7   Check the return value of new.

When new can't allocate the memory you request, it returns 0. Deep in your heart of hearts, you know that checking new's return value is the only truly moral course of action. At the same time, however, you are keenly aware of the fact that writing such tests is a pain in the neck. As a result, chances are that you omit such tests from time to time. Like always, perhaps. Still, you must harbor a lurking sense of guilt. I mean, what if new really *does* return 0?

You may think that one reasonable way to cope with this matter is to fall back on your days in the gutter, i.e., to use the preprocessor. For example, a common C idiom is to define a type-independent macro to allocate memory and then check to make sure the allocation succeeded. For C++, such a macro might look something like this:

```
#define NEW(PTR, TYPE)    \
    (PTR) = new TYPE;      \
    assert((PTR) != 0)
```

("What's this assert business?," you ask. If you look in the standard C include file <assert.h>, you'll see that it's just a macro that checks to see if the expression it's passed is true, and, if it's not, issues an error message and calls abort.)

This NEW macro is fine as far as it goes, but it goes nowhere near far enough. In particular, it fails to take into account the myriad ways in which new can be called. There are three common calling forms for getting new objects of type T, and you need to check the return value for each of these forms:

```
new T;

new T(constructor arguments);

new T[size];
```

This oversimplifies the problem, however, because clients can define their own (overloaded) versions of new at both global and class scope, so any given program could contain an arbitrary number of different versions of new.

How, then, to cope? If you're willing to settle for a very simple error-handling strategy, you can set things up so that if any form of new ever returns 0, a global error-handling function will be called. This strategy relies on the convention that when new cannot satisfy a request, it calls a client-specifiable error-handling function before it returns 0. (In truth, what new really does is slightly more complicated. Details are provided in Item 8.)

To specify the error-handling function, clients call set_new_handler, which is specified in the header file <new.h> as follows:

```
extern void (*set_new_handler (void (*)())) ();
```

Don't panic, now, this isn't as gruesome as it looks. Well, okay, maybe it is, but it's not too difficult to decipher if you put your mind to it. This just says that set_new_handler is a function that takes one argument and returns one result, and both the argument and the result are themselves (pointers to) functions, each of which takes no arguments and returns nothing (i.e., void). Now, then, that wasn't so bad, was it?

The argument to set_new_handler is a pointer to the function that new should call if it can't find the requested memory, and the return value from set_new_handler is a pointer to the function that was in effect for that purpose before set_new_handler was called. That allows you to set up stacks of error-handling functions, a facility you'll exploit below.

You use set_new_handler like this:

```
// function to call if new can't allocate enough memory
void noMoreMemory()
{
  cerr << "Unable to satisfy request for memory\n";
  abort();
}

main()
{
  set_new_handler(noMoreMemory);
  char *bigString = new char[100000000];

  ...

}
```

If, as seems likely, new is unable to allocate space for 100000000 characters, noMoreMemory will be called, and the program will abort after issuing an error message. (Of course, the error message is probably completely meaningless to users, but that's a different topic entirely. This is a marginally better way to terminate the program than a simple core dump.)

Sometimes you'd like to handle memory allocation failures in different ways, depending on the class of the objects that are being allocated:

```
class X {
public:
  static void outOfMemory();

  ...

};
class Y {
public:
  static void outOfMemory();

  ...

};
X* p1 = new X;                  // if unsuccessful,
                                // call X::outOfMemory

Y* p2 = new Y;                  // if unsuccessful,
                                // call Y::outOfMemory
```

Fortunately, it's not too difficult to arrange for this kind of behavior. You just have each class provide its own versions of set_new_handler and operator new.

You'll need to refer to the functions taken and returned by set_new_-handler in the code that follows, so it's convenient to have a typedef for a function that takes no arguments and returns void:

```
typedef void (*PEHF)();         // PEHF = pointer to error
                                // handling function
```

If you have a class X, then, for which you want to handle memory allocation failures, you'll have to keep track of the function to call when new can't allocate the requested memory. Because you want to use the same error-handling function for all members of the class, you'll declare a static member of type PEHF. Your class X will look something like this:

```
class X {
private:
  static PEHF currentPEHF;

public:
  static PEHF set_new_handler(PEHF p);
  void * operator new(size_t size);
};
```

Static class members must be defined outside the class declaration, and because you want to use the default initialization of static objects to 0, you'll define X::currentPEHF without initializing it:

```
PEHF X::currentPEHF;              // sets currentPEHF to 0
                                  // by default
```

The set_new_handler function in class X will just save whatever pointer is passed to it, and it will return whatever pointer had been saved prior to the call. This is exactly what the global version of set_new_handler does:

```
PEHF X::set_new_handler(PEHF p)
{
  PEHF oldPEHF = currentPEHF;
  currentPEHF = p;
  return oldPEHF;
}
```

Finally, X's operator new will simply call the global set_new_handler with X's error-handling function, then will call the global operator new to actually allocate the requested memory, and finally will call the global set_new_handler again to restore the global error-handling function to what it was originally. Notice how you explicitly reference the global scope by using the ":::" notation:

```
void * X::operator new(size_t size)
{
  PEHF currentHandler = ::set_new_handler(currentPEHF);
  void *memory = ::new char[size];
  ::set_new_handler(currentHandler);
  return memory;
}
```

You may note that the code for implementing this scheme is the same regardless of the class, so you might think that this would be a good place to use templates (see Item 49). Unfortunately, it's not legal to write a template for a member function inside a non-template class, so if you want to replicate this code inside every class, you'll have to use the preprocessor. Oh well.

If you're thinking of writing your own versions of new, it might behoove you to take a look at Items 8 and 9. For example, Item 8 explains why you need to ask for an array of chars inside X's operator new.

8   Adhere to convention when writing new.

When you take it upon yourself to write operator new, it's important that your function(s) offer behavior that is consistent with the default new. In practical terms, that means having the right return value, and calling an error-handling function when insufficient memory is available (see Item 7). You also need to avoid inadvertently shadowing the global new, but that's the topic of Item 9.

The return value part is easy. If you can supply the requested memory, you just return a pointer to it. If you can't, you return 0.

It's not quite that simple, however, because new actually tries to allocate memory more than once, calling the error-handling function after each failure, the assumption being that the error-handling function might be able to do something to free up some more memory. Only when the pointer to the error-handling function is 0 does new itself return 0 when it fails to find enough memory.

The pseudocode for a global operator new looks like this; see Item 7 for details on set_new_handler:

```
typedef void (*PEHF)();           // PEHF = pointer to error
                                  // handling function

void * operator new(size_t size)
     // your operator new could
     // take additional params
{
  while (1) {
    attempt to allocate size bytes;

    if (the allocation was successful)
      return (a pointer to the memory);

    // allocation was unsuccessful; find out what the
    // current error-handling function is
    PEHF currentHandler = set_new_handler(0);
    set_new_handler(currentHandler);

    if (currentHandler)
      (*currentHandler)();
    else
      return 0;
  } // end while
}
```

You may look askance at the place in this function where the error-handling function pointer is set to 0, then promptly reset to what it was originally. Unfortunately, there is no way to get at the error-handling function pointer directly, so you have to call set_new_handler to find out what it is. Crude, yes, but also effective.

One of the things that many people don't realize about operator new is that it's inherited by subclasses. That can lead to some interesting complications. In the pseudocode for operator new above, notice that the function tries to allocate size bytes. That makes perfect sense, because that's the argument that was passed into the function. However, most class-specific versions of operator new are designed for a *specific* class, *not* for a class *or* any of its subclasses. That is, given an operator new for a class X, the behavior of that function is almost always carefully tuned for objects of size sizeof(X), nothing larger and nothing smaller. Because of inheritance, however, it is possible that the operator new in a base class will be called to allocate memory for an object of a derived class:

```
class Base {
public:
  void * operator new(size_t size);

  ...

};

class Derived: public Base      // Derived doesn't define
{ ... };                        // operator new

Derived *p = new Derived;       // calls Base::operator new!
```

If Base's class-specific operator new wasn't designed to cope with this — and the chances are very slim that it was — the best way to handle the situation is to slough off all calls requesting the "wrong" amount of memory to the global operator new, like this:

```
void * Base::operator new(size_t size)
{
  if (size != sizeof(Base))      // if size is "wrong"
    return ::new char[size];     // have ::new handle request

  ...                            // otherwise handle request
                                 // here
}
```

It may seem a bit odd to ask the global new for an array of chars if you receive a request for the "wrong" amount of memory. After all, you know that you're really being asked for enough memory for an object of a class derived from Base. However, you also know that this object — whatever its class — takes up size units of memory, and you further know that the units of memory are defined by size_t. Finally, you know that C++ guarantees that sizeof(char) is 1. All that leads you to know that the amount of memory needed for an object of size size is precisely the same as that needed for an array of size characters. See how much you know?

By the way, if you'd like to take over memory allocation for arrays on a per-class basis, you can forget about it right now. The memory for dynamically allocated arrays is *always* allocated by the global operator new:

```
Base *array1 = new Base[10];    // calls ::new because it's
                                // an array

X *array2 = new X[1];           // a 1-element array is
                                // still an array, so this
                                // calls ::new, too
```

9   Avoid hiding the global new.

A declaration of a name in an inner scope hides the same name in outer scopes, so for a function f at both global and class scope, the member function will hide the global function:

```
void f();                       // global function

class X {
public:
  void f();                     // member function
};

X x;

f();                            // calls global f

x.f();                          // calls X::f
```

This is unsurprising and normally causes no confusion, because global and member functions are usually invoked using different syntactic forms. However, if to this class you add an operator new taking additional parameters, the result is likely to be an eye-opener:

```
typedef void (*PEHF)();         // PEHF = pointer to error
                                // handling function

class X {
public:
  void f();

  // operator new allowing specification of
  // error-handling function
  void * operator new(size_t size, PEHF pehf);
};

void specialErrorHandler();     // definition is elsewhere

X *px1 =
  new (specialErrorHandler) X;  // calls X::operator new

X *px2 = new X;                 // error!
```

By defining a function called "operator new" inside the class, you inadvertently block access to the "usual" form of new. Why this is so is discussed in Item 50; here we're more interested in figuring out how to avoid the problem.

One solution is to ask clients to explicitly qualify calls to the global new,

```
X *px2 = ::new X;                    // explicitly call global
                                     // new
```

but such use is unintuitive, and this might come back to haunt you if you later decide you want to write a class-specific new that takes only the size_t argument (because explicitly qualified calls to ::new would bypass any class-specific versions).

A better solution is to write a class-specific operator new supporting the same form as the global new. If it does the same thing as the global new, that can be efficiently and elegantly encapsulated as an inline function:

```
class X {
public:
  void f();

  void * operator new(size_t size, PEHF pehf);

  void * operator new(size_t size)
  { return ::new char[size]; }
};

X *px1 =
  new (specialErrorHandler) X;  // calls X::operator
                                // new(size_t, PEHF)

X* px2 = new X;                 // calls X::operator
                                // new(size_t)
```

Notice that if you later decide to customize the behavior of the "usual" form of new, all you need do is rewrite the function; callers will get the customized behavior automatically when they recompile.

10 Write delete if you write new.

Let's step back for a moment and return to first principles. Why would anybody want to write their own version of new or delete in the first place?

More often than not, the answer is efficiency. The default versions of new and delete are perfectly adequate for general-purpose use, but their wide applicability inevitably leaves room for some improvement in their speed and memory utilization. This is especially true for applications that dynamically allocate a large number of small objects.

As an example, consider a class for representing airplanes, where the Airplane class contains only a pointer to the actual representation for airplane objects (a technique discussed at length in Item 34):

```
class AirplaneRep { ... };      // representation for an
                                // Airplane object
class Airplane {
private:
  AirplaneRep *rep;             // pointer to representation

public:

  ...

};
```

An `Airplane` object is not very big; it contains but a single pointer. (As explained in Item 14, however, it may implicitly contain a second pointer if the `Airplane` class declares any virtual functions.) When you allocate an `Airplane` object by calling `operator new`, however, you probably get back much more memory than is needed to store this pointer (or pair of pointers). The reason for this seemingly wayward behavior has to do with the need for `new` and `delete` to communicate with each other.

Because the default version of `new` is a *general-purpose* allocator, it must be prepared to allocate blocks of any size. Similarly, the default version of `delete` must be prepared to deallocate blocks of whatever size `new` allocated. In order for `delete` to know how much memory to deallocate, it must have some way of knowing how much memory `new` allocated in the first place. The most common way for `new` to tell `delete` how much memory it allocated is by prepending to the memory it returns some additional data that specifies the size of the allocated block. That is, when you say this,

```
Airplane *pa = new Airplane;
```

you don't get back a block of memory that looks like this:

Instead, you get back a block of memory that looks more like this:

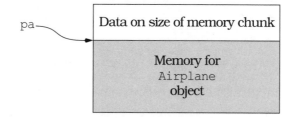

For small objects like those of class `Airplane`, this additional book-keeping data can more than double the amount of memory needed for each dynamically allocated object (especially if the class contains no virtual functions).

If you're developing software for an environment in which memory is precious, you may not be able to afford this kind of spendthrift allocation. By writing your own `operator new` for the `Airplane` class, you can take advantage of the fact that all `Airplane` objects are the same size, so there isn't any need for bookkeeping information to be kept with each allocated block.

One way to implement your class-specific `new` is to ask the default (global) `new` for big blocks of untyped memory, each block of sufficient size to hold a large number of `Airplane` objects. The memory chunks for `Airplane` objects themselves will be organized within the big block as a linked list, using the space for the `rep` field as the link between chunks. In order for this to work, `Airplane*` pointers must be the same size as `AirplaneRep*` pointers; this is the case on most machines.

To institute this strategy, the first thing you have to do is modify the declaration of the `Airplane` class to support memory management. You need to add a declaration for `operator new`, and, in this case, a static pointer to keep track of the head of the linked list of free memory chunks:

```
class Airplane {
private:
  AirplaneRep *rep;
  static Airplane *headOfFreeList;

public:
  void * operator new(size_t size);

  ...

};
```

The next thing is to write the new new:

```
void * Airplane::operator new(size_t size)
{
  // send requests of "wrong" size to ::new (see Item 8)
  if (size != sizeof(Airplane))
    return ::new char[size];

  Airplane *p =                  // p is a pointer into the
    headOfFreeList;              // free list
```

```
// if p is valid, just move the list head to the next
// element in the free list
if (p)
  headOfFreeList = (Airplane*) p->rep;
else {
  // allocate enough memory for 256 Airplane objects
  Airplane *newBlock =
    (Airplane*) ::new char[256 * sizeof(Airplane)];

  // link the memory chunks together through the rep field
  for (int i = 0; i < 255; i++)
    newBlock[i].rep = (AirplaneRep*) &newBlock[i+1];

  // terminate the linked list with a null pointer
  newBlock[255].rep = 0;

  // set p to front of list, headOfFreeList to
  // chunk immediately following
  p = newBlock;
  headOfFreeList = &newBlock[1];
}

  return p;
}
```

Notice how the rep field serves double duty. Within a constructed Airplane object, it holds an AirplaneRep* pointer, so that's how it's declared in the class. However, for memory chunks on the Airplane free list, the rep field isn't inside a constructed object, so you use its space for the pointer to the next element of the free list, which is defined to be an Airplane* pointer. In order to keep the compiler from griping about this inconsistency, you have to use the explicit casts shown in the code. If you didn't already have a pointer in your class, of course, you'd have to add one to support the linked list operations.

Notice also how newBlock is assigned its memory: by requesting an array of chars and then casting the result to be an Airplane* pointer. You might have thought to write this instead,

```
Airplane *newBlock = new Airplane[256];
```

but that does more than allocate memory — it also calls constructors for the elements of the array. In this case, you only want raw memory; you do *not* want constructors to be called.

Finally, notice how the size of each allocated block is hardwired to be enough memory for 256 Airplane objects. Magic numbers like "256" are always a bad idea; a symbolic constant is much better engineering. One straightforward way to handle this matter is to define a global constant (see Item 1), but in this case, a class-specific constant is probably more appropriate, a topic that is examined in laborious detail in Item 32.

The only thing left to do is to provide the obligatory definition of Airplane's static member:

```
// set head of free list to null
Airplane *Airplane::headOfFreeList;
```

There's no need to provide an initial value, because static members are initialized to 0 by default.

This version of new will work just fine. Not only will it use less memory for Airplane objects than does the default new, it's also likely to be faster, possibly as much as two or three times faster. That shouldn't be surprising. After all, the general version of new has to cope with memory requests of different sizes, has to worry about machine-dependent alignment restrictions, etc., whereas your version of new just manipulates a couple of pointers in a linked list. It's easy to be fast when you don't have to be flexible.

At long last we are in a position to discuss operator delete. Remember operator delete? This item is *about* operator delete. As currently written, the Airplane class defines new but does not define delete. Now consider what happens when a client writes the following, which is nothing if not eminently reasonable:

```
Airplane *pa = new Airplane;    // calls
                                // Airplane::operator new
...
delete pa;                      // calls ::delete
```

If you listen closely when you read this code, you can hear the sound of an airplane crashing and burning, with much weeping and wailing by the programmers who knew it. The problem is that new (the one defined in class Airplane) returns a pointer to memory *without any header information*, but delete (the default, global one) assumes that the memory it's passed *does* contain header information! Surely this is a recipe for disaster.

Another way of looking at it is this. Airplane's new is returning a pointer to an element of an array, because Airplane's new calls ::new to get enough room for 256 Airplane objects. However, it *never* makes sense to call delete on the individual elements of a dynamically allocated array, only on the array *in its entirety*.

This example illustrates the general rule: new and delete must be written in concert so that they share the same assumptions. If you're going to roll your own memory allocation routine(s), be sure to roll one for deallocation, too.

Here's how you solve the problem with the Airplane class:

```
class Airplane {

    ...                                        // same as before

public:
    void * operator new(size_t size);
    void operator delete(void *deadObject, size_t size);

    ...

};
// delete is passed a memory chunk, which, if it's the
// right size, is just added to the front of the list of
// free chunks
void Airplane::operator delete(void *deadObject,
                               size_t size)
{
    // send objects of "wrong" size to ::delete
    if (size != sizeof(Airplane)) {
        ::delete [] ((char*) deadObject);
        return;
    }

    Airplane *carcass = (Airplane*) deadObject;
    carcass->rep = (AirplaneRep*) headOfFreeList;
    headOfFreeList = carcass;
}
```

In the same way that you had to use casts inside new to make rep point to different types of objects, you have to use one inside delete, too. Similarly, because you were careful in your hand-crafted version of operator new to ensure that calls of the "wrong" size were forwarded to the global operator new (see Item 8), you must demonstrate equal care in ensuring that such "improperly sized" objects are handled by the global version of operator delete. If you did not, you'd run into precisely the problem you have been laboring so arduously to avoid — a mismatch between new and delete. Finally, because you used [] when calling the global new, you use [] when calling the global delete (see Item 5), and you cast deadObject back to a char* pointer, because that's what the global new originally gave you.

Constructors, Destructors, and Assignment Operators

Almost every class you write will have one or more constructors, a destructor, and an assignment operator. Little wonder. These are your bread-and-butter functions, the ones that control the fundamental operations of bringing a new object into existence and making sure it's initialized correctly; getting rid of an object and making sure that it's been properly cleaned up after; and giving an object a new value. Making mistakes in these functions will lead to far-reaching and distinctly unpleasant repercussions throughout your classes, so it's vital that you get them right. In this section, I offer guidance on putting together the functions that comprise the backbone of well-formed classes.

11 Define a copy constructor and an assignment operator for classes with dynamically allocated memory.

Consider a class for representing String objects:

```
class String {
private:
  char *data;

public:
  String(const char *value = 0);
  ~String();
};

String::String(const char *value)
{
  if (value) {
    data = new char[strlen(value) + 1];
    strcpy(data, value);
  }
  else {
```

```
        data = new char[1];
        *data = '\0';
    }
}

inline String::~String() { delete [] data; }
```

Note that there is no assignment operator or copy constructor declared in this class. As you'll soon see, this has some unfortunate consequences.

If you make these declarations,

```
String a("Hello");
String b("World");
```

then the situation is as shown below:

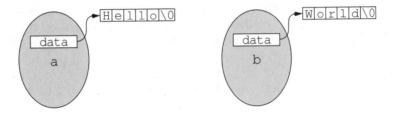

Inside the object a is a pointer to memory containing the character string "Hello". Separate from that is an object b containing a pointer to the character string "World". If you now perform an assignment,

```
b = a;
```

there is no client-defined operator= to call, so C++ generates and calls the default assignment operator instead (see Item 45). This default assignment operator performs memberwise assignment from the members of a to the members of b, which for pointers (a.data and b.data) is just a bitwise copy. The result of this assignment is shown below.

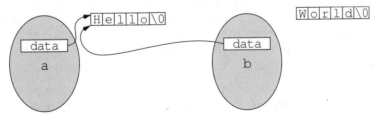

There are at least two problems with this state of affairs. First, the memory that b used to point to was never deleted; it is lost forever. This is a classic example of how a memory leak can arise. Second, both a and b now contain pointers to the same character string. When one of them goes out of scope, its destructor will delete the memory still pointed to by the other. For example:

```
String a("Hello");            // declare and construct a
{                             // open new scope
  String b("World");          // declare and construct b

  ...

  b = a;                      // execute default op=,
                              // lose b's memory

}                             // close scope, call b's
                              // destructor

String c = a;                 // c.data is undefined;
                              // a.data is already deleted
```

The last statement in this example is a call to the copy constructor, which also isn't defined in the class, hence will be generated by C++ in the same manner as the assignment operator (again, see Item 45) and with the same behavior: bitwise copy of the underlying pointers. That leads to the same kind of problem, but without the worry of a memory leak, because the object being initialized can't yet point to any allocated memory.

The case of the copy constructor is a little different, however, because of the way it can bite you: pass-by-value. Of course, Item 22 demonstrates that you should only rarely pass objects by value, but consider this anyway:

```
void doNothing(String localString) {}

String s = "Goodbye cruel world";

doNothing(s);
```

Everything looks innocuous enough, but because localString is passed by value, it must be initialized from s via the (default) copy constructor. Hence localString has a copy of the *pointer* that is inside s. When doNothing finishes executing, localString goes out of scope, and its destructor is called. The end result is by now familiar: s contains a pointer to memory that localString has already deleted.

By the way, the result of calling delete on a pointer that has already been deleted is undefined, so even if s is never used again, there could be a problem when it goes out of scope.

The solution to these kinds of pointer aliasing problems is to write your own versions of the copy constructor and the assignment operator if you have any pointers in your class. Inside those functions you can either copy the pointed-to data structures so that every object has its own copy, or you can implement some kind of reference-counting scheme to keep track of how many objects are currently pointing to a particular data structure. The reference-counting approach is more complicated, and it calls for extra work inside the constructors and destructors, too, but in some (but by no means all) applications it can result in significant memory savings and substantial increases in speed.

Notice one other thing about this class. In the constructor body, I was careful to use [] with new both times I called it, even though in one of the places I only wanted a single object. As is described in Item 5, it's essential to use the same form for corresponding calls to new and delete, so I was careful to be consistent in my calls to new. This is something you do not want to forget. *Always* make sure that you use [] with delete if and only if you used [] with the corresponding call to new.

12 Prefer initialization to assignment in constructors.

Consider a class that allows a name to be associated with arbitrary data:

```
class NamedData {
private:
  String name;
  void *data;

public:
  NamedData(const String& initName, void *dataPtr);
};
```

(In light of the aliasing that can arise during the assignment and copy construction of objects with pointer members (see Item 11), you might wish to consider whether NamedData should implement these functions. Hint: it should (see Item 27).)

When you write the NamedData constructor, you have to transfer the values of the parameters to the corresponding data members. There are two ways to do this. The first way is to use the member initialization list:

```
NamedData::NamedData(const String& initName, void *dataPtr)
: name(initName), data(dataPtr)
{}
```

The second way is to make assignments in the constructor body:

```
NamedData::NamedData(const String& initName, void *dataPtr)
{
  name = initName;
  data = dataPtr;
}
```

There are important differences between these two approaches.

From a purely pragmatic point of view, there are times when the initialization list *must* be used. In particular, const and reference members can *only* be initialized, never assigned. So, if you decided that a NamedData object could never change its name or its data, you might follow the advice of Item 21 and declare the members const:

```
class NamedData {
private:
  const String name;
  void * const data;

public:
  NamedData(const String& initName, void *dataPtr);
};
```

This class declaration *requires* that you use a member initialization list, because const members can *only* be initialized, never assigned.

Very different behavior would be obtained if you decided that a Named-Data object should contain a *reference* to an existing name. Even so, you'd still have to initialize the reference on the constructors' member initialization lists. Of course, you could also combine the two, yielding NamedData objects with read-only access to names that might be modified outside the class:

```
class NamedData {
private:
  const String& name;            // must be initialized on
                                 // initializer list

  void * const data;             // must be initialized on
                                 // initializer list
public:
  NamedData(const String& initName, void *dataPtr);
};
```

The original class, however, contained no const or reference members. Even so, using the member initialization list is still preferable to performing assignments inside the constructor. This time the reason is efficiency. When the member initialization list is used, only a single String member function is called. When assignment inside the constructor is used, two are called. To understand why, consider what happens when you declare a NamedData object.

Construction of objects proceeds in two phases:

1. Initialization of data members in the order of their declaration in the class. (See also Item 13.)

2. Execution of the body of the constructor that was called.

(For objects with base classes, base class member initialization and constructor body execution occurs prior to that for derived classes.)

For the NamedData class, this means that a constructor for the String object name will *always* be called before you ever get inside the body of the NamedData constructor. The only question, then, is this: which String constructor will be called?

That depends on the member initialization list in the NamedData class. If you fail to specify an initialization argument for name, then the default String constructor will be called. When you later perform an assignment to name inside the NamedData constructor, you will call operator= on name. That will make two calls to String member functions: one for the default constructor and one more for the assignment.

On the other hand, if you use the member initialization list to specify that name should be initialized with initName, then name will be initialized through the copy constructor, at a cost of only a single function call.

In the case of the String class, the cost of an unnecessary function call is unlikely to be significant, but as classes become larger and more complex, so do their constructors, and so does the cost of constructing objects. If you establish the habit of using the member initialization list whenever you can, not only do you satisfy a requirement for const and reference members, you minimize the chances of initializing data members in an inefficient manner.

There is, however, one time when it may make sense to use assignment instead of initialization for the data members in a class, and that is when you have a *large number* of data members of *built-in types*, and you want them all initialized the same way in each constructor. For example, here's a class that might qualify for this kind of treatment:

```
class ManyDataMbrs {
private:
  int a, b, c, d, e, f, g, h;
  double i, j, k, l, m;
```

```
public:
  // default constructor
  ManyDataMbrs();

  // copy constructor
  ManyDataMbrs(const ManyDataMbrs& x);
};
```

Suppose you want to initialize all the ints to 1 and all the doubles to 0, even if the copy constructor is used. Using memberwise initialization lists, you'd have to write this:

```
ManyDataMbrs::ManyDataMbrs()
: a(1), b(1), c(1), d(1), e(1), f(1), g(1), h(1), i(0),
  j(0), k(0), l(0), m(0)
{ ... }

ManyDataMbrs::ManyDataMbrs(const ManyDataMbrs& x)
: a(1), b(1), c(1), d(1), e(1), f(1), g(1), h(1), i(0),
  j(0), k(0), l(0), m(0)
{ ... }
```

This is more than just unpleasant drudge work, it is error-prone in the short term and difficult to maintain in the long term.

However, you can take advantage of the fact that there is no operational difference between initialization and assignment for (non-const, non-reference) objects of built-in types, so you can safely replace the memberwise initialization lists with a function call to a common initialization routine:

```
class ManyDataMbrs {
private:
  int a, b, c, d, e, f, g, h;
  double i, j, k, l, m;

  void init();                    // used to initialize data
                                  // members
public:
  // default constructor
  ManyDataMbrs();

  // copy constructor
  ManyDataMbrs(const ManyDataMbrs& x);
};

void ManyDataMbrs::init()
{
  a = b = c = d = e = f = g = h = 1;
  i = j = k = l = m = 0;
}
```

```
ManyDataMbrs::ManyDataMbrs()
{
  init();

  ...

}

ManyDataMbrs::ManyDataMbrs(const ManyDataMbrs& x)
{
  init();

  ...

}
```

Because the initialization routine is an implementation detail of the class, you are, of course, careful to make it private, right?

13 List members in an initialization list in the order in which they are declared.

Unrepentant Pascal and Ada programmers often yearn for the ability to define arrays with arbitrary bounds, i.e., from 10 to 20 instead of from 0 to 10. Longtime C programmers will insist that everybody who's anybody will always start counting from 0, but it's easy enough to placate the begin/end crowd. All you have to do is define your own Array class:

```
class Array {
private:
  int *data;               // ptr to actual array data
  unsigned size;           // # of elements in array
  int lBound, hBound;      // lower bound, higher bound
public:
  Array(int lowBound, int highBound);
};

Array::Array(int lowBound, int highBound)
: size(highBound - lowBound + 1), lBound(lowBound),
  hBound(highBound), data(new int[size])
{}
```

An industrial-strength constructor would perform sanity checking on its parameters to ensure that highBound was at least as great as low-Bound, and of course you should check the return from new to make sure you didn't run out of memory (see Item 7), but there is a much nastier error here: regardless of what new returns, you have absolutely no idea how much memory data points to.

"How can that be?" I hear you cry. "I carefully initialized `size` before calling `new`!" Unfortunately, you didn't, you just tried to. The rules of the game are that class members are initialized *in the order of their declaration in the class*; the order in which they are listed in a member initialization list makes not a whit of difference. In your `Array` class, `data` will always be initialized first, followed by `size`, `lBound`, and `hBound`. No exceptions.

Perverse though this may seem, there is a reason for it. Consider this scenario:

```
class Wacko {
private:
  String s1, s2;

public:
  Wacko(char *s): s1(s), s2(0) {}
  Wacko(const Wacko& x): s2(x.s1), s1(0) {}
};

Wacko w1 = "Hello world!";
Wacko w2 = w1;
```

If members were initialized in the order of their appearance in an initialization list, then the data members of `w1` and `w2` would be constructed in different orders. Recall that the destructors for an object are always called in the inverse order of its constructors. Thus, if the above were allowed, the compiler would have to keep track of the order in which the fields were initialized for *each object*, just to ensure that the destructors would be called in the right order. That would be an expensive proposition. To avoid that overhead, the order of construction and destruction is the same for all objects of a given type, and the order of members in an initialization list is ignored.

Actually, if you really want to get picky about it, only nonstatic data members are initialized according to the rule. Static data members act like global objects, so they are initialized only once; see Item 47 for all the details.

The bottom line is this: if you hope to understand what is really going on when your objects are initialized, be sure to list the members in an initialization list in the order in which those members are declared in the class.

14 Make destructors virtual in base classes.

Sometimes it's convenient for a class to keep track of how many objects of its type are currently in existence. The straightforward way to do this is to create a static class member for counting the objects. The member is initialized to 0, is incremented in the class constructors, and is decremented in the class destructor.

You might envision a military application, in which a class representing enemy targets might look something like this:

```
class EnemyTarget {
private:
  static unsigned numTargets;   // object counter

public:
  EnemyTarget() { numTargets++; }
  ~EnemyTarget() { numTargets--; }

  static unsigned numberOfTargets()
  { return numTargets; }

  virtual Boolean destroy();    // returns success of
                                // attempt to destroy
                                // EnemyTarget object
};

// class statics must be defined outside the class;
// initialization is to 0 by default
unsigned EnemyTarget::numTargets;
```

This class is unlikely to win you a government defense contract, but it will suffice for our purposes here, which are substantially less demanding than are those of the Department of Defense. Or so we may hope.

Let us suppose that a particular kind of enemy target is an enemy tank, which you model, naturally enough (see Item 35), as a publicly derived class of EnemyTarget. Because you are interested in the total number of enemy tanks as well as the total number of enemy targets, you'll pull the same trick with the derived class that you did with the base class:

```
class EnemyTank: public EnemyTarget {
private:
  static unsigned numTanks;     // object counter for tanks

public:
  EnemyTank() { numTanks++; }
  ~EnemyTank() { numTanks--; }

  static unsigned numberofTanks()
  { return numTanks; }

  virtual Boolean destroy();
};
```

Finally, let's assume that somewhere in your application, you dynamically create an EnemyTank object using new, which you later get rid of by calling delete:

```
EnemyTarget *targetPtr = new EnemyTank;

...

delete targetPtr;
```

Everything you've done so far seems completely kosher. Both classes undo in the destructor what they did in the constructor, and there's certainly nothing wrong with your application, in which you were careful to call delete after you were done with the object that you conjured up with new. Nevertheless, there is something very worrisome here. The EnemyTank destructor will never be called. As a result, your count of the number of EnemyTank objects will be incorrect.

The cause of the problem is the call to delete. As you know, when a pointer is deleted, two things happen (see Item 5). First, one or more destructors is called. Second, memory is reclaimed. In your application, you took advantage of the fact that you can initialize an Enemy-Target* pointer (targetPtr) with an EnemyTank* pointer, but this later forced the compiler to face a vexing question: when the Enemy-Target* pointer is deleted, which destructors should be called? You and I know that the pointer *really* points to an EnemyTank object, but how is the compiler supposed to know that? The fact is that it doesn't, so it only calls the destructor for the base class — EnemyTarget in this example.

To avoid this problem, you have only to make the EnemyTarget destructor *virtual*. Declaring the destructor virtual will cause C++ to treat a call to the destructor as it would any other virtual function. Namely, it will call the destructor in the class to which the pointer (or reference) *really* points (or refers). The only difference is that once it has called the destructor in the most derived class, it will *continue to call destructors* all the way up the inheritance graph. When it has finished, a destructor will have been called for each class from which the object in question inherits. In other words, by declaring the destructor virtual in the base class, you tell the compiler that it must examine the object being deleted to see where to start calling destructors.

The EnemyTarget class contains a virtual function, which is generally the case with base classes. After all, the purpose of virtual functions is to allow customization of behavior in derived classes (see Item 36), so almost all base classes contain virtual functions.

If a class does *not* contain any virtual functions, that is often an indication that it is not meant to be used as a base class. When a class is not intended to be used as a base class, making the destructor virtual is usually a bad idea. Consider this example, taken from the ARM (see Item 50):

```
// class for representing 2D points
class Point {
private:
  int x, y;

public:
  Point(int xCoord, int yCoord);
  ~Point();
};
```

If an `int` is represented in 16 bits, a `Point` object can fit into a 32-bit register. Furthermore, a `Point` object can be passed as a 32-bit quantity to functions written in other languages such as C or FORTRAN. If `Point`'s destructor is made virtual, however, the situation changes drastically.

The implementation of virtual functions requires that objects carry around with them some additional information that can be used at runtime to determine which virtual functions should be invoked on the object. In most compilers, this extra information takes the form of a pointer, called a `vptr` ("virtual table pointer"). The `vptr` points to an array of function pointers called a `vtbl` ("virtual table"); each class with virtual functions has an associated `vtbl`. When a virtual function is invoked on an object, the actual function called is determined by following the object's `vptr` to a `vtbl` and then looking up the appropriate function pointer in the `vtbl`.

The details of how virtual functions are implemented are unimportant (and implementation-dependent). What *is* important is that if the `Point` class contains a virtual function, objects of that type will implicitly *double* in size, from two 16-bit `int`s to two 16-bit `int`s plus a 32-bit `vptr`! No longer will `Point` objects fit in a 32-bit register. Furthermore, `Point` objects in C++ no longer look like the same structure declared in another language such as C, because their foreign language counterparts will lack the `vptr`. As a result, it is no longer possible to pass `Point`s to and from functions written in other languages unless you explicitly compensate for the `vptr`, which is itself an implementation detail and hence unportable.

The bottom line is that gratuitously declaring all destructors virtual is just as wrong as never declaring them virtual. In fact, many people summarize the situation this way: declare a virtual destructor in a class if and only if that class contains at least one virtual function.

This is a good rule, one that works most of the time, but unfortunately, it is possible to get bitten by the destructor problem even in the absence of virtual functions. For example, Item 13 considers a class for implementing arrays with client-defined bounds. Suppose that you decide to write a subclass representing named arrays, i.e., a class in which every array has a name of type char*:

```
class Array {                        // base class (from Item 13)
private:
  int *data;
  unsigned size;
  int lBound, hBound;

public:
  Array(int lowBound, int highBound);
  ~Array();
};

class NamedArray: public Array {
private:
  const char * const arrayName;

public:
  NamedArray( int lowBound, int highBound,
             const char *name);
  ~NamedArray();
};
```

Notice that both classes contain nonvirtual destructors, a sure sign of trouble. In the Array constructor, memory will be allocated for the data pointer, and that memory will be deallocated in the Array destructor. In the NamedArray constructor, memory will be allocated for the arrayName pointer, and that memory will be deallocated in the NamedArray destructor. Clearly, you're back in the same situation you had before, even though there are no virtual functions in the base class. If anywhere in an application you somehow convert a pointer-to-NamedArray into a pointer-to-Array, and you then call delete on the Array pointer, you will have a memory leak, because the NamedArray destructor will never be called:

```
NamedArray *pna = new NamedArray(10, 20, "Impending Doom");

Array *pa;

...

pa = pna;                              // NamedArray* -> Array*

...

delete pa;
```

This situation can arise more frequently than you might imagine, because it's not uncommon to want to take an existing class that does something, Array in this case, and derive from it a class that does all the same things, plus more. NamedArray doesn't redefine any of the behavior of Array — it inherits all its functions without change — it just adds some additional capabilities. Yet the destructor problem persists.

In truth, the root cause of all this destructor unpleasantness is poor software design, because Array's destructor is a nonvirtual function, and NamedArray redefines that nonvirtual function, i.e., writes its own destructor. This is nearly always a mistake, a point that is doggedly pursued in Item 37.

Finally, it's worth mentioning that it can be convenient to declare pure virtual destructors in some classes. Recall that pure virtual functions result in *abstract* classes — classes which can't be instantiated (i.e., you can't create objects of that type). Sometimes, however, you have a class that you'd like to be abstract, but you don't happen to have any functions that are pure virtual. What to do? Well, because an abstract class is intended to be used as a base class, and because a base class should have a virtual destructor, and because a pure virtual function yields an abstract class, the solution is simple: declare a pure virtual destructor in the class you want to be abstract.

Here's an example:

```
class AWOV {                    // AWOV = "Abstract w/o
                                // Virtuals"
public:
  virtual ~AWOV() = 0;          // declare pure virtual
                                // destructor
};
```

This class has a pure virtual function, so it's abstract, and it has a virtual destructor, so you can rest assured that you won't have to worry about the destructor problem. There is one twist, however: you *must* provide a *definition* for the pure virtual destructor:

```
AWOV::~AWOV() {}                 // definition of pure
                                 // virtual destructor
```

You need this definition because the way virtual destructors work, remember, is that the most derived class's destructor is called first, then the destructor of each base class is called. That means that the compiler will generate a call to ~AWOV even though the class is abstract, so you have to be sure to provide a body for the function. If you don't, the linker will probably complain about a missing symbol, and you'll have to go back and add one.

You can do anything you like in that function, but, as in the example above, it's not uncommon to have nothing to do. If that is the case, you'll probably be tempted to avoid paying the overhead cost of a call to an empty function by declaring your destructor inline. This seems like a perfectly sensible strategy, but since when does perfect sense count?

Because your destructor is virtual, its address will be entered into the class's vtbl. Because inline functions aren't supposed to exist (that's what inline means, right?), special measures must be taken to get addresses for them. The whole tawdry story is spelled out in Item 33, but the moral of the tale is this: if you declare your virtual destructor inline, you may well end up paying for a function call each time it's invoked, and your overall code size will probably increase, too.

15 Have operator= return a reference to *this.

Bjarne Stroustrup, the designer of C++, went to a lot of trouble to ensure that user-defined types would mimic the built-in types as closely as possible. That's why you can overload operators, write type conversion functions, take control of assignment and copy construction, etc. After so much effort on his part, the least you can do is keep the ball rolling.

Which brings us to assignment. With the built-in types, you can chain assignments together, like so:

```
int w, x, y, z;

w = x = y = z = 0;
```

As a result, you should be able to chain together assignments for user-defined types, too:

```
class String {
private:
  char *data;

public:
  String(const char *value = 0);
};

String w, x, y, z;

w = x = y = z = "Hello";
```

As fate would have it, the assignment operator is right-associative, so the assignment chain is parsed like this:

```
w = (x = (y = (z = "Hello")));
```

It's worthwhile to write this in its completely equivalent functional form. Unless you're an underground LISP programmer, this example should make you grateful for the ability to define infix operators.

```
w.operator=(x.operator=(y.operator=(z.operator=("Hello"))));
```

This form is illustrative because it emphasizes that the argument to `w.operator=`, `x.operator=`, and `y.operator=` is the return value of a previous call to `operator=`. As a result, the return type of `opera-tor=` must also be acceptable as an input to itself. For the default version of `operator=` in a class `C`, the signature of the function is as follows (see Item 45):

```
C& C::operator=(const C&);
```

You'll almost always want to follow this convention of having `opera-tor=` both take and return a reference to a class object, although at times you may overload `operator=` so that it takes different argument types. For example, `String` classes often have at least two different versions of the assignment operator:

```
String&                        // assign a String
operator=(const String&);      // to a String

String&                        // assign a char*
operator=(const char*);        // to a String
```

Even in the presence of overloading, however, notice that the return type is a reference to an object of the class.

A common error amongst new C++ programmers is to have `operator=` return void, a decision that seems reasonable until you realize that it prevents chains of assignment. So don't do it.

Within an assignment operator bearing the default signature, there are two obvious candidates for the object to return: the object on the left hand side of the assignment (the one pointed to by `this`) and the object on the right-hand side (the one named in the parameter list). Which is correct?

Here are the possibilities for the `String` class (a class for which you'll definitely want to write an assignment operator, as explained in Item 11):

```
String& String::operator=(const String& rhs)
{

   ...

   return *this;                  // return reference
                                  // to left-hand object
}
```

```
String& String::operator=(const String& rhs)
{

  ...

  return rhs;                      // return reference to
                                   // right-hand object
}
```

This might strike you as a case of six of one versus a half a dozen of the other, but there actually are important differences.

First, the version returning `rhs` won't compile. That's because `rhs` is a reference-to-*const*-`String`, but `operator=` returns a reference-to-`String`, and the compiler will give you no end of grief for trying to return a non-`const` reference to a `const` object. That's easy enough to get around, however — just redeclare `operator=` like this:

```
String& String::operator=(String& rhs) { ... }
```

Now a more serious problem becomes apparent. Consider part of the original chain of assignments:

```
x = "Hello";                      // same as x.op=("Hello");
```

Because the right-hand argument of the assignment is not of the correct type — it's a `char*`, not a `String` — the compiler creates a temporary `String` object via the `String` constructor, then calls the assignment operator with the temporary. It's roughly the same as this:

```
String temp("Hello");            // create temporary

x = temp;                        // pass temporary to op=
```

The crucial question is this: what is the life-span of the temporary that the compiler generated? In particular, when will it be destroyed?

Frankly, you don't know. You know that it will exist for the duration of the call to `operator=`, but after that, all bets are off. That leads to the disquieting possibility that in the expression

```
x = y = "Hello";                  // x.op=(y.op=("Hello"))
```

the temporary created for the call to `y.operator=` will be destroyed before it is passed into the call to `x.operator=`. If that happens, what takes place inside `x.operator=` is anybody's guess. This isn't an entirely theoretical concern — I know at least one compiler that actually exhibits this (entirely legal) behavior.

You thus find yourself in the happy circumstance of having no choice whatsoever: you'll always want to define your assignment operators in such a way that they return a reference to their left-hand argument, `*this`. Not only does this protect you from the when-does-the-temporary-get-destroyed problem, it also allows you to declare operator='s parameter as a reference-to-const, which is safer than just declaring it to be a reference.

16 Assign to all data members in operator=.

Item 45 explains that C++ will write an assignment operator for you if you don't write one yourself, and Item 11 describes why you probably won't much care for the one it writes for you, so perhaps you're wondering if you can't somehow have the best of both worlds, whereby you let C++ generate a default assignment operator and you selectively override those parts you don't like. No such luck. If you want to take control of any part of the assignment process, you must do the entire thing yourself.

In practice, this means that you need to assign to *every* data member of your object when you write your assignment operator(s):

```
// a class for representing geometric points
class Point {
private:
  long x, y;

public:
  Point(long xCoord, long yCoord): x(xCoord), y(yCoord) {}

  Point& operator=(const Point& rhs);

  ...

};

Point& Point::operator=(const Point& rhs)
{
  if (this == &rhs)
    return *this;                    // see Item 17

  // assign to all data members
  x = rhs.x;
  y = rhs.y;

  return *this;                      // see Item 15
}
```

This is easy enough to remember when the class is originally written, but it's equally important that the assignment operator(s) be updated if new data members are added to the class. For example, if you decide to upgrade the Point class to represent three-dimensional coordinates, you'll have to add a new data member, and this will require updating the constructor(s) as well as the assignment operator(s). In the hustle and bustle of upgrading a class and adding new member functions, etc., it's easy to let this kind of thing slip your mind.

The real fun begins when inheritance joins the party, however, because a derived class's assignment operator(s) must also handle assignment of its base class members! Consider this:

```
class A {
private:
  int x;

public:
  A(int initialValue): x(initialValue) {}
};

class B: public A {
private:
  int y;

public:
  B(int initialValue): A(initialValue), y(initialValue) {}

  B& operator=(const B& rhs);
};
```

The logical way to write B's assignment operator is like this:

```
// erroneous assignment operator
B& B::operator=(const B& rhs)
{
  if (this == &rhs) return *this;

  y = rhs.y;

  return *this;
}
```

Unfortunately, this doesn't work, because the data member x in the A part of a B object is unaffected by this assignment operator. Here's a little test program you can use to prove it:

```
main()
{
  B b0(0);              // b0.x = 0, b0.y = 0
  B b1(1);              // b1.x = 1, b1.y = 1

  b0 = b1;              // b0.x = 0, b0.y = 1!
}
```

Notice how the A part of b0 is unchanged by the assignment.

The straightforward way to fix this problem would be to make an assignment to x in B::operator=. Unfortunately, that's not legal, because x is a private member of A. Instead, you have to make an explicit assignment to the A *part* of B from inside B's assignment operator.

This is how you do it:

```
// correct assignment operator
B& B::operator=(const B& rhs)
{
  if (this == &rhs) return *this;

  ((A&) *this) = rhs;             // call operator= on
                                  // A part of *this

  y = rhs.y;

  return *this;
}
```

This monstrosity casts *this to be a reference to an A, then makes an assignment to the result of the cast. That makes an assignment to only the A part of the B object. Careful now! It is important that the cast be to a *reference* to an A object, not to an A object itself. If you cast *this to be an A object, you'll end up calling the copy constructor for A, and the new object you construct will be the target of the assignment; *this will remain unchanged. Hardly what you want.

If, as is commonly the case, the base class explicitly declares an assignment operator, a less intimidating-looking way to accomplish the same thing is as follows:

```
class A {                        // same as above, but with
public:                          // op= explicitly declared
  A& operator=(const A& rhs);

  ...

};

class B: public A { ... };       // same as above

B& B::operator=(const B& rhs)
{
  if (this == &rhs) return *this;

  A::operator=(rhs);             // call this->A::operator=
  y = rhs.y;

  return *this;
}
```

Here you just make an explicit call to A::operator=. That call, like all calls to member functions from within other member functions, will use *this as its implicit left-hand object. The result will be that A::operator= will do whatever work it does on the A part of *this, precisely the effect you want.

Regardless of which of these approaches you employ, once you've assigned the A part of the B object, you then continue with B's assignment operator, making assignments to all the data members of B.

17 Check for assignment to self in `operator=`.

An assignment to self is when you do something like this:

```
class X { ... };

X a;

a = a;                          // a is assigned to itself
```

This looks like a silly thing to do, but it's perfectly legal, so don't doubt for a moment that programmers do it. More importantly, assignment to self can appear in this more benign looking form:

```
a = b;
```

If `b` is another name for `a` (for example, a reference that has been initialized to `a`), then this is also an assignment to self, though it doesn't outwardly look like it. This is an example of *aliasing*: having two or more names for the same underlying object. As you'll see at the end of this item, aliasing can crop up in any number of nefarious disguises, so you need to take it into account any time you write a function.

Two good reasons exist for taking special care to cope with possible aliasing in assignment operator(s). One of them is efficiency. If you can detect an assignment to self at the top of your assignment operator(s), you can return right away, possibly saving a lot of work that you'd otherwise have to go through to implement assignment. For example, Item 16 points out that a proper assignment operator in a derived class must call an assignment operator for each of its base classes, and those classes might themselves be derived classes, so skipping the body of an assignment operator in a derived class might save a large number of other function calls.

A more important reason for checking for assignment to self is that of correctness. Remember that an assignment operator must typically free the resources allocated to an object (i.e., get rid of its old value) before it can allocate the new resources corresponding to its new value. When assigning to self, this freeing of resources can be disastrous, because the old resources might be needed during the process of allocating the new ones.

Consider assignment of `String` objects, where the assignment operator fails to check for assignment to self:

```
class String {
private:
  char *data;
```

```
public:
  String(const char *value = 0);
                                    // see Item 11 for function
                                    // definition

  ~String();                        // see Item 11 for function
                                    // definition

  String& operator=(const String& rhs);
};

// an assignment operator that omits a check
// for assignment to self
String& String::operator=(const String& rhs)
{
  delete [] data;                   // delete old memory

  // allocate new memory and copy old data into it
  data = new char[strlen(rhs.data) + 1];
  strcpy(data, rhs.data);

  return *this;                     // see Item 15
}
```

Consider now what happens in this case:

```
String a = "Hello";

a = a;                              // same as a.operator=(a)
```

Inside the assignment operator, *this and rhs seem to be different objects, but in this case they happen to be different names for the same object. You can envision it like this:

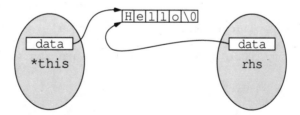

The first thing the assignment operator does is call delete, and the result is the following state of affairs:

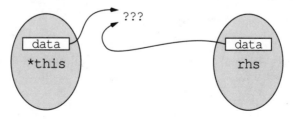

Now when the assignment operator tries to do a `strlen` on `rhs.data`, the results are undefined. This occurs because `rhs.data` was deleted when `data` was deleted, which happened because `data`, `this->data`, and `rhs.data` are all the same pointer! From this point on, things can only get worse.

By now you know that the solution to the dilemma is to check for an assignment to self and to return immediately if such an assignment is detected. Unfortunately, it's much easier to talk about such a check than it is to write it, because you are immediately forced to figure out what it means for two objects to be "the same."

The topic you confront is technically known as that of *object identity*, and it's an active topic in object-oriented research circles. This book is no place for a discourse on object identity, but it is worthwhile to mention the two basic approaches to the problem.

One approach is to say that two objects are the same (have the same identity) if they have the same value. For example, two `String` objects would be the same if they represented the same sequence of characters:

```
String a = "Hello";
String b = "World";
String c = "Hello";
```

Here a and c have the same value, so they are considered identical; b is different from both of them. If you wanted to use this definition of identity in your `String` class, your assignment operator might look like this:

```
String& String::operator=(const String& rhs)
{
  if (strcmp(data, rhs.data) == 0) return *this;

  ...

}
```

Value equality is usually determined by `operator==`, so the general form for an assignment operator for a class C that uses value equality for object identity is this:

```
C& C::operator=(const C& rhs)
{
  // check for assignment to self
  if (*this == rhs)                    // assumes op== exists
    return *this;

  ...

}
```

Note that this function is comparing *objects* (via operator==), not pointers. Using value equality to determine identity, it doesn't matter whether two objects occupy the same memory; all that matters is the values they represent.

The other possibility is to equate an object's identity with its address in memory. Using this definition of object equality, two objects are the same if and only if they have the same address. This definition is more common in C++ programs, probably because it's easy to implement and the computation is fast, neither of which is always true when object identity is based on values. Using address equality, a general assignment operator looks like this:

```
C& C::operator=(const C& rhs)
{
  // check for assignment to self
  if (this == &rhs) return *this;

  ...

}
```

This is fairly reliable, but *only* if you limit yourself to single inheritance (not that that's a bad idea — see Item 43.) The minute you start to use multiple inheritance, you must steel yourself for the fact that a single object can have more than one address, regardless of whether you are using virtual or nonvirtual base classes. Here's an example, both in C++ and in a graphical notation that uses arrows running from base classes to derived classes:

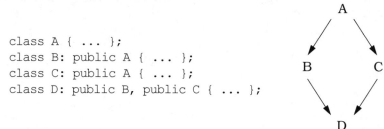

```
class A { ... };
class B: public A { ... };
class C: public A { ... };
class D: public B, public C { ... };
```

If you create an object of class D, that object may have up to five different addresses, depending on how it's used:

```
D d;                        // create object of class D

D* pD1 = &d;                // pD1 is address of D
                            // part of d

B* pD2 = &d;                // pD2 is address of B
                            // part of d

C* pD3 = &d;                // pD3 is address of C
                            // part of d
```

```
A* pD4 = (B*) &d;              // pD4 is address of A part
                              // of B part of d

A* pD5 = (C*) &d;              // pD5 is address of A part
                              // of C part of d
```

Each of the five pointers pD1, pD2, pD3, pD4, and pD5 points to the same object — d — but there is no guarantee that any two of the pointers will have the same value. In fact, it's a sure bet that the two different A parts of d will have different addresses. If A were a virtual base class, then d might have only four different addresses, but clearly that wouldn't help the matter of object identity any.

Most programmers eventually conclude that if they want to have a robust mechanism for determining whether two objects are the same, they must implement it themselves. The most common approach is based on a virtual function that returns some kind of object identifier:

```
class C {
public:
  virtual ObjectID identity() const;

  ...

};
```

Given object pointers a and b, then, the objects they point to are identical if and only if a->identity() == b->identity(). Of course, you are responsible for writing operator== for ObjectIDs.

The problems of aliasing and object identity are hardly confined to operator=; that's just a function in which you are particularly likely to run into them. In the presence of references and pointers, any two names for objects of compatible types may in fact refer to the same object. Here are some other situations in which aliasing can show its Medusa-like visage:

```
class Base {
  void mf1(Base& rb);          // rb and *this could be
                              // the same

  ...

};

void f1(Base& rb1,Base& rb2); // rb1 and rb2 could be
                              // the same

class Derived: public Base {
  void mf2(Base& rb);          // rb and *this could be
                              // the same

  ...

};
```

```
int f2(Derived& rd, Base& rb); // rd and rb could be
                               // the same
```

These examples happen to use references, but pointers would serve just as well.

As you can see, aliasing can crop up in a variety of guises, so you cannot just forget about it and hope you'll never run into it. Well, maybe *you* can do that, but most of us can't. At the expense of mixing my metaphors, this is a clear case in which an ounce of prevention is worth its weight in gold. Anytime you write a function in which aliasing could conceivably be present, you *must* take that possibility into account when you write the code. Failure to do so is just *asking* for trouble.

Classes and Functions: Design and Declaration

Declaring a new class in a program creates a new type: class design is *type* design. You probably have little experience with type design, because most languages don't offer you the opportunity to get any practice. In C++, however, it is of fundamental importance, not just because you can do it if you want to, but because you *are* doing it every time you declare a class, whether you mean to or not.

Designing good classes is hard because designing good types is hard. Good types have a natural syntax, intuitive semantics, and one or more efficient implementations. In C++, a poorly thought out class declaration can make it impossible to achieve any of these goals. Even the performance characteristics of a class's member functions are determined as much by the declarations of those member functions as they are by their definitions.

How, then, do you go about designing effective classes? First, you must understand the issues you face. Virtually every class requires that you confront the following questions, the answers to which often lead to subtle constraints on your design:

- *How should objects be created and destroyed?* That exerts a strong influence on the design of your constructors and destructor, as well as your versions of new and delete, if you write them.

- *How does object initialization differ from object assignment?* That determines the behavior of and the differences between your constructors and your assignment operators.

- *What does it mean to pass objects of the new type by value?* As noted in the introduction to this book, the copy constructor defines what it means to pass an object by value.

- *What are the constraints on legal values for the new type?* These constraints determine the kind of error checking you'll have to do inside your member functions, especially your constructors and assignment operators.

- *Does the new type fit into an inheritance graph?* If you inherit from existing classes, you are constrained by the design of those classes, particularly by their choice of whether the functions you inherit are virtual or nonvirtual. If you wish to allow other classes to inherit from your class, that will affect your determination as to whether functions you declare are virtual or not.

- *What kind of type conversions are allowed?* If you wish to allow objects of type A to be *implicitly* converted into objects of type B, then you will want to write either a type conversion function in class A, or a constructor in class B that can be called with a single argument. If you wish to allow *explicit* conversions only, you'll want to write functions to perform the conversions, but you won't want to make them type conversion operators or constructors that can be called with a single argument.

- *What operators and functions make sense for the new type?* The answer to this question determines which functions you'll declare in your class interface.

- *What standard operators and functions should be explicitly disallowed?* Those operators and functions are the ones you'll need to declare private.

- *Who should have access to the members of the new type?* This question helps you determine which members are public, which are protected, and which are private. It also helps you determine which classes and/or functions should be friends.

These are difficult questions, so declaring effective classes in C++ is far from simple. Done properly, however, user-defined classes in C++ can be made all but indistinguishable from built-in types, and that makes all the effort worthwhile.

A discussion of the details of each of the above issues would comprise a book in its own right, so the guidelines that follow are anything but comprehensive. However, they highlight some of the most important design considerations, warn about some of the most common errors, and provide solutions to some of the most common problems encountered by class designers. Much of the advice is as applicable to global functions as it is to member functions, so I consider their design and declaration in this section, too.

18 Strive for class interfaces that are complete and minimal.

The client interface for a class is the interface that is accessible to the programmers who use the class. Typically, only functions exist in this interface, because having data members in the client interface has a number of drawbacks (see Item 20).

Trying to figure out what functions should be in a class interface can drive you crazy. You're pulled in two completely different directions. On the one hand, you'd like to build a class that is easy to understand, straightforward to use, and easy to implement. That usually implies a fairly small number of member functions, each of which performs a distinct task. On other hand, you'd like your class to be powerful and convenient to use, which often means adding functions to provide support for commonly performed tasks. How do you decide which functions go into the class and which ones don't?

Try this: aim for a class interface that is *complete* and *minimal.*

A complete interface is one that allows clients to do anything they might reasonably want to do. That is, for any reasonable task that clients might want to accomplish with an object of the class, there is a reasonable way to accomplish it, although it may not be as convenient as clients might like. A minimal interface, on the other hand, is one with as few functions in it as possible, one in which no two member functions have overlapping functionality. If you offer a complete, minimal interface, clients can do whatever they want to do, but the class interface is no more complicated than absolutely necessary.

The desirability of a complete interface seems obvious enough, but why a minimal interface? Why not just give clients everything they ask for, adding functionality until everyone is happy?

Aside from the moral issue — is it really *right* to mollycoddle your clients? — there are definite technical disadvantages to a class interface that is crowded with functions. First, the more functions in an interface, the harder it is for potential clients to understand. The harder it is for them to understand, the more reluctant they will be to learn how to use it. A class with 20 functions looks tractable to most people, but a class with 100 functions is enough to make many programmers run and hide. By expanding the functionality of your class to make it as attractive as possible, you may actually end up discouraging people from learning how to use it.

A large interface can also lead to confusion. Suppose you create a class that supports cognition for an artificial intelligence application. One of your member functions is called `think`, but you later discover that some people want the function to be called ponder, and others prefer the name ruminate. In an effort to be accommodating, you offer all three functions, even though they do the same thing. Consider then the plight of a potential client of your class who is trying to figure things out. The client is faced with three different functions, all of which are supposed to do the same thing. Can that really be true? Isn't there some subtle difference between the three, possibly in efficiency or generality or reliability? If not, why are there three different functions? Rather than appreciating your flexibility, such a potential client is likely to wonder what on earth you were thinking (or pondering, or ruminating over).

A second disadvantage to a large class interface is that of maintenance. It's simply more difficult to maintain and enhance a class with many functions than it is a class with few. It is more difficult to avoid duplicated code (with the attendant duplicated bugs), and it is more difficult to maintain consistency across the interface.

Finally, long class declarations result in long header files, and because header files typically have to be read every time a program is compiled (see Item 34), class declarations that are longer than necessary can incur a substantial penalty in total compile-time over the life of a project.

The long and short of it is that the gratuitous addition of functions to an interface is not without costs, so you need to think carefully about whether the convenience of a new function (a new function can *only* be added for convenience if the interface is already complete) justifies the additional costs in complexity, comprehensibility, maintainability, and compilation speed.

Yet there's no sense in being unduly miserly. It is often justifiable to offer more than a minimal set of functions. If a commonly performed task can be implemented much more efficiently as a member function, that may well justify its addition to the interface. If the addition of a member function makes the class substantially easier to use, that may be enough to warrant its inclusion in the class. And if adding a member function is likely to prevent client errors, that, too, is a powerful argument for its being part of the interface.

Consider a concrete example, a class that implements arrays with client-defined upper and lower bounds and that offers optional bounds-checking. Such a class would be useful for holding any type of object, so you'll declare it as a template. (If you're unfamiliar with templates, take a look at Item 49. If your compiler doesn't support templates yet, you can use the preprocessor to simulate them (see Item 1).)

The beginning of such an array class is shown below:

```
template<class T>
class Array {
public:
  enum BoundsCheckingStatus {NO_CHECK_BOUNDS = 0,
                             CHECK_BOUNDS = 1};

private:
  int lBound, hBound;           // low bound, high bound

  T *data;                      // ptr to array contents

  BoundsCheckingStatus checkingBounds;
public:
  Array(int lowBound, int highBound,
        BoundsCheckingStatus check = NO_CHECK_BOUNDS);

  Array(const Array& rhs);

  ~Array();

  Array& operator=(const Array& rhs);
};
```

The member functions declared so far are the ones that require basically no thinking (or pondering or ruminating). You have a constructor to allow clients to specify each array's bounds, and because you have dynamically allocated memory (the data pointer), you know you'll need a copy constructor and an assignment operator (see Item 11); you will also need a destructor to deallocate the memory that will be allocated in the constructors (see Item 6). In this case, you've declared the destructor nonvirtual, which implies that this class is not to be used as a base class (see Item 14).

The declaration of the assignment operator is actually less clear-cut than it might at first appear. After all, built-in arrays in C++ don't allow assignment, so you might want to disallow it for your Array objects, too (see Item 27). In this example, however, you choose to allow assignment, which, as you'll see below, will have an impact on other portions of the class interface.

Old-time C hacks would cringe to see this interface — where is the support for declaring an array of a particular size? It would be easy enough to add another constructor,

```
Array(int size,
      BoundsCheckingStatus check = NO_CHECK_BOUNDS);
```

but this is not part of a minimal interface, because the constructor taking an upper and lower bound can be used to accomplish the same thing. Nonetheless, it might be a wise political move to humor the old geezers, possibly under the rubric of consistency with the base language.

What other functions do you need? Certainly it is part of a complete interface to index into an array:

```
// return element for read/write
T& operator[](int index);

// return element for read-only
const T& operator[](int index) const;
```

By declaring the same function twice, once `const` and once non-const, you provide support for both `const` and non-const `Array` objects. The difference in return types is significant, as is explained in Item 21.

As it now stands, the `Array` class supports construction, destruction, pass-by-value, assignment, and indexing, which may strike you as a complete interface. But look closer. Suppose a client wants to loop through an array of integers, printing out each of its elements, like so:

```
Array<int> a(10, 20);          // bounds on a are 10 to 20

...

for (int i = lower bound of a; i <= upper bound of a; i++)
    cout << "a[" << i << "] = " << a[i] << '\n';
```

How is the client to get the bounds of a? The answer depends very much on what happens during assignment of `Array` objects, i.e., on what happens inside `Array::operator=`. In particular, if assignment can change the bounds of an `Array` object, you must provide member functions to return the current bounds, because the client has no way of knowing *a priori* what the bounds are at any given point in the program. In the example above, if a was the target of an assignment between the time it was declared and the time it was used in the loop, the client would have no way to determine the current bounds of a.

On the other hand, if the bounds of an `Array` object cannot be changed during assignment, then the bounds are fixed at the point of declaration, and it would be possible (though cumbersome) for a client to keep track of these bounds. In that case, though it would be convenient to offer functions to return the current bounds, such functions would not be part of a truly minimal interface.

Proceeding on the assumption that assignment can modify the bounds of an object, the bounds functions could be declared thus:

```
int lowBound() const;
int highBound() const;
```

Because these functions don't modify the object on which they are invoked, and because you prefer to use const whenever you can (see Item 21), these are both declared const member functions. Given these functions, the loop above would be written as follows:

```
for (int i = a.lowBound(); i <= a.highBound(); i++)
    cout << "a[" << i << "] = " << a[i] << '\n';
```

Needless to say, for such a loop to work for an array of objects of type T, an operator<< function must be defined for objects of type T.

Some designers would argue that the Array class should also offer a function to return the number of elements in an Array object. The number of elements is simply highBound()-lowBound()+1, so such a function is entirely unnecessary, but in view of the frequency of off-by-one errors, it might not be a bad idea to add such a function.

Other functions that might prove worthwhile for this class include those for input and output, as well as the various relational operators (e.g., <, >, ==, etc.). None of those functions is part of a minimal interface, however, because they can all be implemented in terms of loops containing calls to operator[].

Speaking of functions like operator<<, operator>>, and the relational operators, Item 19 discusses why they are frequently implemented as global friend functions instead of as member functions. That being the case, don't forget that friend functions are, for all practical purposes, part of a class's interface. That means that friend functions count toward a class interface's completeness and minimalness.

19 Differentiate among member functions, global functions, and friend functions.

The biggest difference between member functions and global functions is that member functions can be virtual and global functions can't. As a result, if you have a function that has to be dynamically bound (see Item 38), then you've got to use a virtual function, and that virtual function must be a member of some class; it's as simple as that. If your function doesn't need to be virtual, however, the water begins to muddy a bit.

Consider a class for representing rational numbers:

```
class Rational {
private:

    ...
```

```
public:
  Rational(int numerator = 0, int denominator = 1);
  int numerator() const;
  int denominator() const;
};
```

As it stands now, this is a pretty useless class. (Using the terms of Item 18, the interface is certainly minimal, but it's *far* from complete.) You know that you'd like to support arithmetic operations like addition, subtraction, multiplication, etc., but you're unsure whether you should use a member function or a global function, or possibly a global function that's a friend.

When in doubt, be object-oriented. You know that, say, multiplication of rational numbers is related to the Rational class, so try bundling the operation with the class by making it a member function:

```
class Rational {
public:

  ...

  Rational operator*(const Rational& rhs) const;
};
```

(If you're unsure why this function is declared the way it is — returning its result by value, but taking a reference-to-constant as its argument — consult Items 23 and 22, respectively.)

Now you can multiply rational numbers with the greatest of ease:

```
Rational oneEighth(1, 8);
Rational oneHalf(1, 2);

Rational result =
  oneHalf * oneEighth;          // fine

result = result * oneEighth;    // fine
```

But you're not satisfied. You'd also like to support mixed-mode operations, where Rationals can be multiplied with, for example, ints. When you try to do this, however, you find that it works only half the time:

```
result = oneHalf * 2;           // fine

result = 2 * oneHalf;           // error!
```

This is a very bad omen. Multiplication is supposed to be commutative, remember?

The source of the problem becomes apparent when you rewrite the last two examples in their equivalent functional form:

```
result = oneHalf.operator*(2); // fine
result = 2.operator*(oneHalf); // error!
```

The object `oneHalf` is an instance of a class that contains an `operator*`, so the compiler calls that function. However, the integer 2 has no associated class, hence no `operator*` member function. The compiler also looks for a global `operator*` that can be called like this,

```
result = operator*(2, oneHalf);// error!
```

but there is no global `operator*` taking an `int` and a `Rational`, so the search fails.

Look again at the call that succeeds. You'll see that its second parameter is the integer 2, yet `Rational::operator*` takes a `Rational` object as its argument. What's going on here? Why does 2 work in one position and not in the other?

What's going on is implicit type conversion. The compiler knows that you're passing an `int` and that the function requires a `Rational`, but it also knows that it can conjure up an appropriate `Rational` by calling the `Rational` constructor with the `int` you provided, so that's what it does. In other words, it treats the call as if it had been written like this:

```
Rational temp(2);              // turn 2 into a Rational
result = oneHalf * temp;       // same as
                               // oneHalf.operator*(temp);
```

In fact, your handy-dandy compiler will perform this kind of implicit type conversion, if it's needed, on *every* parameter of *every* function call. However, it will do it only for parameters *listed in the parameter list*; *never* for the object on which a member function is invoked, i.e., the object corresponding to `*this` inside a member function. That's why this call works,

```
result = oneHalf.operator*(2); // converts int -> Rational
```

and this one does not:

```
result = 2.operator*(oneHalf); // doesn't convert
                               // int -> Rational
```

The first case involves a parameter listed in the function declaration and the second one does not.

Nonetheless, you'd still like to support mixed-mode arithmetic, and the way to do it is by now perhaps clear: make `operator*` a global function, thus allowing the compiler to perform implicit type conversions on *all* arguments:

```
class Rational {

   ...                                    // contains no operator*

};

Rational operator*(const Rational& lhs, const Rational& rhs)
{
   return Rational(lhs.numerator() * rhs.numerator(),
                   lhs.denominator() * rhs.denominator());
}

Rational oneFourth(1, 4);
Rational result;

result = oneFourth * 2;      // fine
result = 2 * oneFourth;      // hooray, it works!
```

This is certainly a happy ending to the tale, but there is a nagging worry. Should operator* be made a friend of the Rational class?

In this case, the answer is no, because operator* can be implemented entirely in terms of the class's public interface. The code above shows one way to do it. However, it's not uncommon for functions that are global, yet still conceptually part of a class interface, to need access to the non-public members of the class.

As an example, let's fall back on a workhorse of this book, the String class. If you try to overload operator>> and operator<< for reading and writing String objects, you'll quickly discover that they shouldn't be member functions. If they were, you'd have to put the String object on the left when you called the functions:

```
// a class declaration that mistakenly declares
// operator>> and operator<< as member functions
class String {
private:
  char *data;

public:
  String(const char *value = 0);

   ...

  istream& operator>>(istream& input);
  ostream& operator<<(ostream& output);
};
```

```
String s;

s >> cin;                          // legal, but contrary
                                   // to convention

s << cout;            .            // ditto
```

That would confuse everyone. As a result, these functions shouldn't be member functions, they should be global. Notice that this is a different case than we discussed above. Here the goal is a natural calling syntax; earlier we were concerned about implicit type conversions.

If you were designing these functions, you'd come up with something like this:

```
istream& operator>>(istream& input, String& string)
{
  delete [] string.data;

  read from input into some memory, and make string.data
  point to it

  return input;
}

ostream& operator<<(ostream& output,
                    const String& string)
{
  return output << string.data;
}
```

Notice that both functions need access to the `data` field of the `String` class, a field that's private. However, you already know that you have to make them global functions. You're boxed into a corner and you have no choice: global functions with a need for access to non-public members of a class must be made friends of that class.

The lessons of this item are summarized in the following pseudocode, in which it is assumed that `f` is the function you're trying to declare properly and `C` is the class to which it is conceptually related:

```
// virtual functions must be members
if (f needs to be virtual)
  make f a member function of C;

// operator>> and operator<< are never members
else if (f is operator>> or operator<<) {
  make f a global function;
  if (f needs access to non-public members of C)
    make f a friend of C;
  }
```

```
// only nonmembers can have type conversions on
// their left-most argument
else if (f needs type conversions on its
          left-most argument) {
  make f a global function;
  if (f needs access to non-public members of C))
    make f a friend of C;
  }
// everything else should be a member function
else
  make f a member function of C;
```

20 Avoid data members in the public interface.

First, let's look at this issue from the point of view of consistency. If everything in the public interface is a function, clients of your class won't have to scratch their heads trying to remember whether to use parentheses when they want to access a member of your class. They'll just *do* it, because everything is a function. Over the course of a lifetime, that can save a lot of head scratching.

You don't buy the consistency argument? How about the fact that using functions gives you much more precise control over the accessibility of data members? If you make a data member public, everybody has read/write access to it, but if you use functions to get and set its value, you can implement no access, read-only access, and read-write access. Heck, you can even implement write-only access if you want to (useful for modeling APL source code):

```
class AccessLevels {
private:
  int noAccess;                // no access to this int

  int readOnly;                // read-only access to
                               // this int

  int readWrite;               // read-write access to
                               // this int

  int writeOnly;               // write-only access to
                               // this int
public:
  int getReadOnly() const{ return readOnly; }

  void setReadWrite(int value){ readWrite = value; }
  int getReadWrite() const{ return readWrite; }

  void setWriteOnly(int value){ writeOnly = value; }
};
```

Still not convinced? Then it's time to bring out the big gun: functional abstraction. If you implement access to a data member through a function, then you can later replace the data member with a computation, and nobody using your class will be any the wiser.

For example, suppose you are writing an application in which some automated equipment is monitoring the speed of passing cars. As each car passes, its speed is computed, and the value is added to a collection of all the speed data collected so far:

```
class SpeedDataCollection {
public:
  void addValue(int speed);       // add a new data value

  double averageSoFar() const;  // return average speed
};
```

Now consider the implementation of the member function `averageSoFar`. One way to implement it is to have a data member in the class that is a running average of all the speed data so far collected. Whenever `averageSoFar` is called, it just returns the value of that data member. A different approach is to have `averageSoFar` compute its value anew each time it's called, something it could do by examining each data value in the collection.

The first approach — keeping a running average — makes each `SpeedDataCollection` object bigger, because you have to allocate space for the data member holding the running average, but `averageSoFar` can be implemented very efficiently: it's just an inline function that returns the value of the data member. Conversely, computing the average whenever it's requested will make `averageSoFar` run slower, but each `SpeedDataCollection` object will be smaller.

Who's to say which is best? On a machine where memory is tight, and in an application where averages are needed only infrequently, computing the average each time is a better solution. In an application where averages are needed frequently, speed is of the essence, and memory is not an issue, keeping a running average is preferable. The important point is that by accessing the average through a member function, you can use *either* implementation, a valuable source of flexibility that you wouldn't have if you made a decision to include the running average data member in the public interface.

The upshot of all this is that you're just *asking* for trouble by putting data members in the public interface, so play it safe by hiding all your data members behind a wall of functional abstraction. If you do it *now*, we'll throw in consistency and fine-grained access control at no extra cost!

21 Use const whenever possible.

The wonderful thing about const is that it allows you to specify a certain semantic constraint — a particular object should *not* be modified — and the compiler will enforce that constraint. It allows you to communicate to both the compiler and to other programmers that a value should remain invariant. Whenever that is true, you should be sure to say so explicitly, because that way you enlist the compiler's aid in making sure the constraint isn't violated.

The const keyword is remarkably versatile. Outside of classes, you can use it for global constants (see Item 1) and for static objects (local to either a file or a block). Inside classes, you can use it for either static or nonstatic data members (see also Item 12), although its use for establishing class-specific constants is somewhat limited (see Item 32).

For pointers, you can specify whether the pointer itself is const, the data it points to is const, both, or neither:

```
char *p          = "Hello";  // non-const pointer,
                             // non-const data

const char *p    = "Hello";  // non-const pointer,
                             // const data

char * const p   = "Hello";  // const pointer,
                             // non-const data

const char * const p= "Hello";  // const pointer,
                             // const data
```

This syntax isn't quite as capricious as it looks. Basically, what you do is mentally draw a vertical line through the asterisk of a pointer declaration, and if the word const appears to the left of the line, what's *pointed to* is constant; if the word const appears to the right of the line, the *pointer itself* is constant; if const appears on both sides of the line, both are constant:

What's pointed to is constant	Pointer is constant
char * p = "Hello";	
const char * p = "Hello";	
char * **const** p = "Hello";	
const char * **const** p = "Hello";	

Some of the most powerful uses of const, however, stem from its application to function declarations. Within a function declaration, const can refer to the function's return value, to individual parameters, and, for member functions, to the function as a whole.

Having a function return a constant value is a great way to achieve both efficiency and safety, topics that are addressed more fully in Items 22 and 29. For example, suppose you have a `String` class that represents its data internally as a `char*`, and you'd like to offer a safe, efficient conversion from a `String` to a `char*`. A nice way to do it is to return a copy of your internal pointer as a *const* `char *`:

```
class String {
private:
  char *data;

public:
  String(const char *value = 0);

  ...

  // returns a copy of an internal pointer,
  // but as a pointer-to-const
  operator const char *() const { return data; }
};
```

There's nothing particularly new about `const` parameters — they act just like local `const` objects. Const member functions, however, are a different story.

The purpose of `const` member functions, of course, is to specify which member functions may be invoked on `const` objects. Many people overlook the fact that member functions differing *only* in their const-ness can be overloaded, however, and this is an important feature of C++. Consider the `String` class once again:

```
class String {
private:
  char *data;

public:

  ...

  // operator[] for non-const objects
  char& operator[](int position)
  { return data[position]; }

  // operator[] for const objects
  const char& operator[](int position) const
  { return data[position]; }
};
String s1 = "Hello";
cout << s1[0];                    // calls non-const
                                  // String::operator[]

const String s2 = "World";
cout << s2[0];                    // calls const
                                  // String::operator[]
```

Okay, so maybe the `operator[]` functions should do some sanity checking on `position` to make sure it's in range. That's not the point here. The point is that by overloading `operator[]` and giving the different versions different return values, you are able to have `const` and non-const `String`s handled differently:

```
String str = "World";          // non-const String object

const String
  constStr = "Hello";          // const String object

char c2 = str[0];              // fine — reading a
                               // non-const String

char c1 = constStr[0];         // fine — reading a
                               // const String

str[0] = 'x';                  // fine — writing a
                               // non-const String

constStr[0] = 'x';             // error! — writing a
                               // const String
```

By the way, note that the error here has only to do with the *return value* of the `operator[]` that is called; the calls to `operator[]` themselves are all fine. The error arises out of an attempt to make an assignment to a `const char&`, because that's the return value from the `const` version of `operator[]`.

Also note that the return value of `operator[]` must be a *reference* to a `char` — a `char` itself simply will not do. If `operator[]` did return a simple `char`, then statements like this wouldn't compile:

```
str[0] = 'x';
```

That's because it's never legal to try to modify the return value of a function. Besides, even if it were legal, the fact that C++ returns objects by value (see Item 22) would mean that a *copy* of `str.data[0]` would be modified, not `str.data[0]` itself, and that's not the behavior you want, anyway.

Let's take a brief time-out for philosophy. What exactly does it mean for a member function to be `const`? There are two prevailing notions: bitwise constness, and conceptual constness.

The bitwise const camp believes that a member function is `const` if and only if it doesn't modify any of the object's data members (excluding those that are static), i.e., if it doesn't modify any of the bits inside the object. The nice thing about bitwise constness is that it's easy to detect violations: the compiler just looks for assignments to data members. In fact, bitwise constness is C++'s definition of constness, and a `const` member function isn't allowed to modify any of the data members of the object on which it is invoked.

Unfortunately, many member functions that don't act very `const` pass the bitwise test. In particular, a member function that modifies what a pointer *points to* frequently doesn't act `const`, but if only the *pointer* is in the object, the function is bitwise const, and the compiler won't complain. That can lead to counterintuitive behavior:

```
class String {
private:
  char *data;

public:
  // the constructor makes data point to a copy
  // of what value points to
  String(const char *value = 0);

  operator char *() const { return data;}
};

const String s = "Hello";       // declare constant object

char *nasty = s;                // calls op char*() const

*nasty = 'M';                   // modifies s.data[0]

cout << s;                      // writes "Mello"
```

Surely there is something wrong when you create a constant object with a particular value and you invoke only `const` member functions on it, yet you are still able to change its value!

This leads to the notion of conceptual constness. Adherents to this philosophy argue that a `const` member function might modify some of the bits in the object on which it's invoked, but only in ways that are undetectable by a client. For example, your `String` class might want to cache the length of the object whenever it's requested:

```
class String {
private:
  char *data;

  unsigned dataLength;       // last calculated length
                             // of string

  unsigned lengthIsValid:1;  // bit indicating if length
                             // is currently valid
public:
  // the constructor makes data point to a copy
  // of what value points to
  String(const char *value = 0): lengthIsValid(0) { ... }
```

```
    unsigned length() const;
};

unsigned String::length() const
{
  if (!lengthIsValid) {
    dataLength = strlen(data);   // error!
    lengthIsValid = 1;           // error!
  }

  return dataLength;
}
```

This implementation of length is certainly not bitwise const — both dataLength and lengthIsValid may be modified — yet it seems as though it should be valid for const String objects. The compiler, you will find, respectfully disagrees; it insists on bitwise constness. What to do?

This brings us at long last to the wonderful world of casting away constness. Inside a member function of class C, the type of the this pointer is as if it had been declared as follows:

```
C * const this;              // for non-const member
                             // functions

const C * const this;        // for const member
                             // functions
```

This is how the compiler actually detects a violation of constness in a const member function: it uses the same rules for the this pointer as it would for any other pointer-to-const.

That being the case, all you have to do to make the above version of String::length valid for both const and non-const objects is to change the type of this from const C * const to C * const. You can't do that directly, but you can fake it by initializing a local pointer to point to the same object as this does. Then you can access the members you want to modify through the local pointer:

```
unsigned String::length() const
{
  // make a local version of this that's
  // not a pointer-to-const
  String * const localThis = (String * const) this;

  if (!lengthIsValid) {
    localThis->dataLength = strlen(data);
    localThis->lengthIsValid = 1;
  }

  return dataLength;
}
```

Pretty this ain't, but sometimes a programmer's just gotta do what a programmer's gotta do.

Unless, of course, it's not guaranteed to work, and sometimes the old cast-away-constness trick isn't. In particular, if the object that `this` points to is in read-only memory, then you can cast until you're blue in the face and you still won't be able to modify `*this`. Fortunately, the conditions under which an object can be placed in read-only memory are well defined. To wit, an object can be placed in read-only memory only if it has no constructors and no destructor. Hence, if you want to cast away constness in one of your member functions, you'd best be sure that the object you're doing the casting on is of a class that declares at least one constructor or destructor.

There is one other time when casting away constness may be both useful and safe. That's when you have a `const` object that you want to pass to a function taking a non-`const` parameter, and *you know that the parameter won't be modified inside the function*. The second condition is important, because it is always safe to cast away the constness of an object that will only be read — not written — even if that object resides in read-only memory.

For example, some libraries have been known to incorrectly declare the `strlen` function as follows:

```
int strlen(char *s);
```

Certainly `strlen` isn't going to modify what s points to — at least not the `strlen` I grew up with. Because of this declaration, however, it would be invalid to call it on pointers of type `const char *`. To get around the problem, you can safely cast away the constness of such pointers when you pass them to `strlen`:

```
const char *greeting = "Hello World";
unsigned length = strlen((char *) greeting);
```

Don't get cavalier about this, though. It is guaranteed to work only if the function being called, `strlen` in this case, doesn't try to modify what its pointer parameter points to.

22 Pass and return objects by reference instead of by value.

In C, everything is passed by value, and C++ honors this heritage by adopting the pass-by-value convention as its default. Unless you specify otherwise, function parameters are initialized with *copies* of the actual arguments, and function callers get back a *copy* of the value returned by the function.

As is pointed out in the introduction, the meaning of passing an object by value is defined by the copy constructor of that object's class. This can make pass-by-value an extremely expensive operation. For example, consider the following (rather contrived) class hierarchy:

```
class String { ... };          // see Item 21 for
                               // possible definition

class Person {
private:
  String name, address;

public:
  Person();                    // parameters omitted for
                               // simplicity

  ~Person();

  ...

};

class Student: public Person {
private:
  String schoolName, schoolAddress;

public:
  Student();                   // parameters omitted for
                               // simplicity

  ~Student();

  ...

};
```

Now consider a simple function returnStudent that takes a Student argument (by value) and immediately returns it (also by value), plus a call to that function:

```
Student returnStudent(Student p)
{
  return p;
}

Student s;

returnStudent(s);
```

What happens during the course of this innocuous-looking function call?

The simple explanation is this: the Student copy constructor is called to initialize p with s. Then the Student copy constructor is called again to initialize the object returned by the function with p. Next, the destructor is called for p. Finally, sometime later, the destructor is called for the object returned by `returnStudent`. So the cost of this do-nothing function is two calls to the `Student` copy constructor and two calls to the `Student` destructor.

But wait, there's more! A `Student` object has two `String` objects within it, so every time you construct a `Student` object you must also construct two `String` objects. A `Student` object also inherits from a `Person` object, so every time you construct a `Student` object you must also construct a `Person` object. A `Person` object has two additional `String` objects inside it, so each `Person` construction also entails two more `String` constructions. The end result is that passing a `Student` object by value leads to one call to the `Student` copy constructor, one call to the `Person` copy constructor, and four calls to the `String` copy constructor. When the copy of the `Student` object goes out of scope, each constructor call is matched by a destructor call, so the overall cost of passing a `Student` by value is six constructors and six destructors. Because the function `returnStudent` uses pass-by-value twice (once for the parameter, once for the return value), the complete cost of a call to that function is *twelve* constructors and *twelve* destructors!

In fairness to the C++ compiler-writers of the world, this is a worst-case scenario. Compilers are allowed to eliminate many of these calls to copy constructors (the ARM — see Item 50 — describes the precise conditions under which they are allowed to perform this kind of magic), and some compilers take advantage of this license to optimize. Until such optimizations become commonplace, however, you've got to be wary of the cost of passing objects by value.

To avoid this potentially exorbitant cost, you need to pass things not by value, but by reference:

```
Student& returnStudent(Student& p) { return p; }
```

This is much more efficient: no constructors or destructors are called, because no new objects are being created.

Passing parameters by reference has another advantage: it avoids what is sometimes called the "slicing problem." When a derived class object is turned into a base class object, all of the specialized features that made it behave like a derived class object are "sliced" off, and you're left with a simple base class object. This is almost never what you want. For example, suppose you're working on a set of classes for implementing a graphical window system:

```
class Window {
public:
  const char * name() const;     // return name of window
  virtual void display() const;// draw window and contents
};
class WindowWithScrollBars: public Window {
public:
  virtual void display() const;
};
```

All `Window` objects have a name, which you can get at through the `name` function, and all windows can be displayed, which you can bring about by invoking the `display` function. The fact that `display` is virtual tells you that the way in which simple base class `Window` objects are displayed is apt to be different from the way in which the fancy, high-priced `WindowWithScrollBars` objects are displayed (see Items 36 and 37).

Now suppose you'd like to write a function to print out a window's name and then display the window. Here's the *wrong* way to write such a function:

```
// a function that suffers from the slicing problem
void printNameAndDisplay(Window w)
{
  cout << w.name();
  w.display();
}
```

Consider what happens when you call this function with a Window-WithScrollBars object:

```
WindowWithScrollBars wwsb;

printNameAndDisplay(wwsb);
```

The parameter w will be constructed — it's passed by value, remember? — as a `Window` object, and all the specialized information that made wwsb act like a `WindowWithScrollBars` object will be sliced off. Inside `printNameAndDisplay`, w will always act like an object of class `Window`, regardless of the type of the object that is passed in to the function. In particular, the call to `display` inside `printNameAndDisplay` will *always* call `Window::display`, never `WindowWithScrollBars::display`.

The way around the slicing problem is to pass w in by reference:

```
// a function that doesn't suffer from the slicing problem
void printNameAndDisplay(const Window& w)
{
  cout << w.name();
  w.display();
}
```

Now w will act like whatever kind of window is actually passed in. To emphasize that w isn't modified by this function even though it's passed by reference, you've carefully declared it to be const; how good of you.

Passing by reference is a wonderful thing, but it leads to certain complications of its own, the most notorious of which is aliasing, a topic that is discussed in Item 17. In addition, it's important to recognize that you sometimes *can't* pass things by reference; see Item 23. Finally, the brutal fact of the matter is that references are almost always implemented as pointers, so passing something by reference usually means really passing a pointer. As a result, if you have a particularly small object — a short, for example — it may actually be more efficient to pass it by value than to pass it by reference.

23 Don't try to return a reference when you must return an object.

It is said that Albert Einstein once offered this advice: make things as simple as possible, but no simpler. The C++ analogue might well be to make things as efficient as possible, but no more efficient.

Once programmers grasp the efficiency implications of pass-by-value for objects (see Item 22), they become crusaders, determined to root out the evil of pass-by-value wherever it may hide. Unrelenting in their pursuit of pass-by-reference purity, they invariably make a fatal mistake: they start to pass references to objects that don't exist. This is not a good thing.

Consider the well-worn example of a class for complex numbers, including a friend function for adding two complex numbers together:

```
class Complex {
private:
  double r, i;                  // real, imaginary parts
                                // of number

public:
  Complex(double realPart = 0, double imagPart = 0);
  ~Complex();
```

```
friend Complex operator+(const Complex& lhs,
                         const Complex& rhs);
};

inline Complex operator+(const Complex& lhs,
                         const Complex& rhs)
{
  return Complex(lhs.r + rhs.r, lhs.i + rhs.i);
}
```

Clearly this version of operator+ is returning its result object by value, and just as clearly — unless you have an unusually aggressive optimizing compiler (and you probably don't) — this means you're going to have to pay the price of a call to the constructor and a call to the destructor for that object. The only thing that could be clearer than these facts is that you're cheap and you don't want to pay if you don't have to. So the question is this: do you have to?

Well, you don't have to if you can return a reference instead. But remember that a reference is just a name, a name for some *existing* object. Whenever you see the declaration for a reference, you should immediately ask yourself what it is another name for, because it must be another name for *something*. In the case of your operator+, if the function is to return a reference, then it must return a reference to some other Complex object that already exists and that contains the sum of the two objects that are to be added together.

There is certainly no reason to expect that such an object exists prior to the call to operator+. That is, if you have

```
Complex a(3, 2);
Complex b(-5, 22);
Complex c = a + b;
```

it seems unreasonable to expect that there already exists a complex number with the value (-2, 24). No, if operator+ is to return a reference to such a number, it must create that number object itself.

A function can create a new object in only two ways: on the stack or on the heap. Creation on the stack is accomplished by defining a local variable. Using that strategy, you might try to write your operator+ as follows:

```
// the first wrong way to write this function
inline
Complex& operator+(const Complex& lhs, const Complex& rhs)
{
  Complex result(lhs.r + rhs.r, lhs.i + rhs.i);
  return result;
}
```

You can reject this approach out of hand, because your goal was to avoid a constructor call, and `result` will have to be constructed just like any other object. In addition, this function has a more serious problem in that it returns a reference to a local object, an error that is discussed in depth in Item 31.

That leaves you with the possibility of constructing an object on the heap and then returning a reference to it. Heap-based objects come into being through calls to `new`. This is how you might write `operator+` in that case:

```
// the second wrong way to write this function
inline
Complex& operator+(const Complex& lhs, const Complex& rhs)
{
  Complex *result =
    new Complex(lhs.r + rhs.r, lhs.i + rhs.i);
  return *result;
}
```

Well, you *still* have to pay for a constructor call, because the memory allocated by `new` is initialized by calling an appropriate constructor (see Item 5), but now you have a different problem: who will call `delete` on the object that was conjured up by your call to `new`?

In fact, this is a guaranteed memory leak. Even if callers of `operator+` could be persuaded to take the address of the function's result and then call `delete` on it (astronomically unlikely), complicated expressions would yield unnamed temporaries that programmers would never be able to get at. For example, in

```
Complex w, x, y, z;

w = x + y + z;
```

both calls to `operator+` yield unnamed temporaries that the programmer never sees.

In the case of an `operator+` for complex numbers, then, as in life itself, there is no free lunch. The function must create a new object, and there is no reasonable way for it to return a reference to this new object. It must return the new object by value, like it or not.

The moral of the story is this: if you need a new object, you're going to have to pay to construct (and destruct) it. If you try to evade the cost, you are going to end up with corrupt data or a memory leak, and you will *still* be hit up for the price of construction. So don't try to duck the cost — pay it up front and get it over with.

24 Choose carefully between function overloading and parameter defaulting.

The confusion over function overloading and parameter defaulting is that they both allow a single function name to be called in more than one way:

```
void f();                       // f is overloaded
void f(int x);

f();                            // calls f()
f(10);                          // calls f(int)

void g(int x = 0);              // g has a default
                                // parameter value

g();                            // calls g(0)
g(10);                          // calls g(10)
```

So which should be used when?

The answer depends on two other questions. First, is there a value that you can use for a default? Second, how many algorithms do you want to use? In general, if you can choose a reasonable default value and you want to employ only a single algorithm, you'll use default parameters (see also Item 38). Otherwise you'll use function overloading.

Here's a function to compute the maximum of up to five ints. This function uses INT_MIN as a default parameter value. You can find the definition for INT_MIN in <limits.h>, part of your friendly neighborhood ANSI C standard include library.

```
int max(int a, int b = INT_MIN, int c = INT_MIN,
        int d = INT_MIN, int e = INT_MIN)
{
  int temp = a > b ? a : b;
  temp = temp > c ? temp : c;
  temp = temp > d ? temp : d;
  return temp > e ? temp : e;
}
```

The crucial observation is that this function uses the same (rather inefficient) algorithm to compute its result, regardless of the number of actual parameters provided by the caller. Nowhere in the function do you attempt to figure out which parameters are "real" and which are defaults. Instead, you have chosen a default value that cannot possibly affect the validity of the computation for the algorithm you're using.

For many functions, there is no reasonable default value. For example, suppose you want to write a function to compute the average (mathematical mean) of up to five ints. You can't use default parameter values here, because the result of the function is dependent on the number of parameters passed in: if 3 values are passed in, you'll divide their sum by 3; if 5 values are passed in, you'll divide their sum by 5. Furthermore, there is no "magic number" you can use as a default to indicate that a parameter wasn't actually provided by the client, because all possible ints are valid values for the parameters. In this case, you have no choice: you *must* use overloaded functions:

```
int avg(int a);
int avg(int a, int b);
int avg(int a, int b, int c);
int avg(int a, int b, int c, int d);
int avg(int a, int b, int c, int d, int e);
```

The other case in which you need to use overloaded functions is when you want to accomplish a particular task, but the algorithm that you use depends on the inputs that are given. This is commonly the case with constructors: a default constructor will construct an object from scratch, whereas a copy constructor will construct one from an existing object:

```
// A class for representing natural numbers
class Natural {
private:
  unsigned value;

  void init(int initValue);
  void error(char *msg);

public:
  Natural(int initValue);
  Natural(const Natural& x);
};

inline
void Natural::init(int initValue) { value = initValue; }

Natural::Natural(int initValue)
{
  if (initValue > 0) init(initValue);
  else error("Illegal initial value");
}

inline Natural::Natural(const Natural& x)
{ init(x.value); }
```

The constructor taking an int has to perform error checking, but the copy constructor doesn't, so two different functions are needed. That means overloading. However, note that both functions must assign an initial value for the new object. This could lead to code duplication in the two constructors, so you maneuver around that problem by writing a private member function init that contains the code common to the two constructors. This tactic — using overloaded functions that call a common underlying function for some of their work — is frequently useful.

This last example also sneaks in a private error-handling function for coping with problems encountered during construction. Because constructors have no return value, trying to deal with errors encountered during construction is awkward and won't really be tractable until exception handling (see Item 49) is commonly available. A complete discussion of the issue is beyond the scope of this book; suffice it to say that a private error-handling function is one of many more or less unsatisfactory ways of tiding us over until exception handling arrives. For other ideas on coping in the meantime, see Item 49.

25 Avoid overloading on a pointer and a numerical type.

Trivia question for the day: what is zero?

More specifically, what will happen here?

```
void f(int x);
void f(char *p);

f(0);                              // calls f(int) or f(char*)?
```

The answer is that 0 is an `int` — a literal integer constant, to be precise — so `f(int)` will always be called. Therein lies the problem, because that's not what people always want. This is a situation unique in the world of C++: a place where people think a call should be ambiguous, but the compiler does not.

It would be nice if you could somehow manage to tiptoe around this problem by use of a symbolic name, say, `NULL` for pointers with value 0, but that turns out to be a lot tougher than you might imagine.

Your first suggestion might be to declare a constant called `NULL`, but constants have types, and what type should `NULL` have? It needs to be compatible with all pointer types, but the only pointer satisfying that requirement is `void*`, and you can't pass `void*` pointers to typed pointers without an explicit cast. Not only is that ugly, at first glance it's not a whole lot better than the original situation:

```
const void * const NULL = 0;

f(0);                              // still calls f(int)
f((char*) NULL);                   // calls f(char*)
f((char*) 0);                      // calls f(char*)
```

On second thought, however, the use of NULL as a void* constant is a shade better than what you started with, because you avoid ambiguity if you use only NULL to indicate pointers with value 0:

```
f(0);                    // calls f(int)
f(NULL);                 // error!
f((char*) NULL);         // calls f(char*)
```

At least now you've traded a runtime error (the call to the "wrong" f for 0) for a compile-time error (the attempt to pass a void* into a char* parameter). This improves matters somewhat (see Item 46), but the cast is still unsatisfying.

If you shamefacedly crawl back to the preprocessor, you find that it doesn't really offer a way out, either, because the only choices seem to be

```
#define NULL 0
#define NULL (void*) 0
```

and the first possibility is just the literal "0," which is fundamentally an integer constant (your original problem, as you'll recall), while the second possibility gets you back into the trouble with passing void* pointers to typed pointers.

In desperation, you might try to combine templates (see Item 49) and user-defined conversion operators to create an object called NULL that can be converted into whatever type of pointer is needed,

```
// a nice idea that won't work
class NullClass {
public:
  template<class T> operator T*() const { return 0; }
};

const NullClass NULL;

// this should call f(NullClass::operator char*(NULL))
f(NULL);
```

but this won't work because templates can be declared only at global scope. Sigh.

What's left is the brute force approach: a different name for each different type of null pointer:

```
const int    * const NULLint    = 0;
const char   * const NULLchar   = 0;
const double * const NULLdouble = 0;
const String * const NULLString = 0;
```

Needless to say, this requires that you create a new NULL every time you create a new type name, a tedious process, though one that is easily automated.

An important point about all these attempts to come up with a workable NULL is that they help you only if you're the *caller*. If you're the *author* of the functions being called, having a foolproof NULL wouldn't help you at all, because you couldn't require that your callers use it. As a designer of overloaded functions, then, the bottom line is that you're best off avoiding overloading on a numerical and a pointer type if you can possibly avoid it.

26 Guard against potential ambiguity.

Everybody has to have a philosophy. Some people believe in *laissez faire* economics, others believe in reincarnation. Some people even believe that COBOL is a real programming language. C++ has a philosophy, too: it believes that potential ambiguity is not an error.

Here's an example of potential ambiguity:

```
class A {
public:
  A(const class B&);          // an A can be
                              // constructed from a B
};
class B {
public:
  operator A() const;         // a B can be
                              // converted to an A
};
```

There's nothing wrong with these class declarations — they can coexist peacefully in the same program without the slightest trouble. However, look what happens when you combine these classes with a function that takes an A object, but is actually passed a B object:

```
void g(const A&);

B b;

g(b);                         // error! − ambiguous
```

Seeing the call to g, the compiler knows that it must somehow come up with an object of type A, even though what it has in hand is an object of type B. There are two equally good ways to do this, however. On one hand, the class A constructor could be called, which would construct a new A object using b as an argument. On the other hand, b could be converted into an A object by calling the client-defined conversion operator in class B. Because these two approaches are considered equally good, the compiler refuses to choose between them.

Of course, it's entirely possible that you'd been using this program for some time without ever having run across the ambiguity. That's the insidious peril of potential ambiguity. It can lie dormant in a program for long periods of time, undetected and inactive, until the day when some unsuspecting programmer does something that actually *is* ambiguous, at which point pandemonium breaks out. This gives rise to the disconcerting possibility that you might release a library that can be called ambiguously without even being aware of the fact that you're doing it.

One of the worst things about potential ambiguity is that programmers who perform the ambiguous action may have no way around the problem — they may be at the mercy of the library they are using. For example, if you didn't have access to the source code of the two classes above, how would you force a call to the A constructor instead of the B type conversion operator?

A similar form of ambiguity arises from standard conversions in the language — you don't even need any classes:

```
void h(int);
void h(char);

double d = 6.02;

h(d);                          // error! — ambiguous
```

Should d be converted into an int or a char? Both are equally good, so the compiler refuses to judge. Fortunately, you can get around this problem by using an explicit cast:

```
h(int(d));                     // fine, calls h(int)
h((char) d);                   // fine, calls h(char)
```

Finally, multiple inheritance (see Item 43) is rife with possibilities for potential ambiguity. The most straightforward case is when a derived class inherits the same member name from more than one base class:

```
class Base1 {
public:
  int doIt();
};
class Base2 {
public:
  void doIt();
};
```

```
class Derived:public Base1,     // Derived doesn't declare
               public Base2 {    // a function called doIt
  ...

};

Derived d;

d.doIt();                        // error! - ambiguous
```

When class `Derived` inherits two functions with the same name, C++ utters not a whimper; at this point the ambiguity is only potential. However, the call to `doIt` forces the compiler to face the issue, and unless you explicitly disambiguate the call by specifying which base class function you want, the call is an error.

```
d.Base1::doIt();                 // fine, calls Base1::doIt

d.Base2::doIt();                 // fine, calls Base2::doIt
```

That doesn't upset too many people, but the fact that accessibility restrictions don't enter into the picture has caused more than one otherwise pacifistic soul to mull over distinctly unpacifistic actions:

```
class Base1 { ... };             // same as above

class Base2 {
private:
  void doIt();                   // this function is now
                                 // private
};

class Derived:public Base1, public Base2
{ ... };                         // same as above

Derived d;

int i = d.doIt();                // error! - still ambiguous!
```

The call to `doIt` continues to be ambiguous, even though only the function in `Base1` is accessible! The fact that only `Base1::doIt` returns a value that can be used to initialize an `int` is also irrelevant — the call remains ambiguous. If you want to make this call, you simply *must* specify which class's `doIt` is the one you want.

As is the case for most initially unintuitive rules in C++, there is a good reason why access restrictions are not taken into account when disambiguating references to multiply inherited members. It boils down to this: changing the accessibility of a class member should never change the meaning of a program.

For example, assume that in the previous example, access restrictions were taken into account. Then the expression `d.doIt()` would resolve to a call to `Base1::doIt`, because `Base2`'s version was inaccessible.

Now assume that Base1 was changed so that its version of doIt was protected instead of public, and Base2 was changed so that its version was public instead of private.

Suddenly the same expression, d.doIt(), would result in a *completely different function call*, even though neither the calling code nor the functions had been modified! Now *that's* unintuitive, and there's no way for the compiler to issue even a warning. Considering your choices, you may decide that having to explicitly disambiguate references to multiply inherited members isn't quite as unreasonable as you originally thought.

Given that there are all these different ways to write programs and libraries harboring potential ambiguity, what's a good software developer to do? Primarily, you need to keep an eye out for it. It's next to impossible to root out all the sources of potential ambiguity, particularly when programmers combine libraries that were developed independently (see also Item 28), but by understanding the situations that often lead to potential ambiguity, you're in a better position to minimize its presence in the software you design and develop.

27 Explicitly disallow use of implicitly generated member functions you don't want.

Suppose you want to write a class Array that behaves like built-in C++ arrays in every way, except it performs bounds checking. One of the design problems you would face is how to prohibit assignment between Array objects, because assignment isn't legal for C++ arrays:

```
char string1[10];
char string2[10];

string1 = string2;              // error!
```

For most functions, this wouldn't be a problem. If you didn't want to allow a function, you simply wouldn't put it in the class. However, the assignment operator is one of those distinguished member functions that C++, always the helpful servant, writes for you if you neglect to write it yourself (see Item 45). What then to do?

The solution is to declare the function, operator= in this case, *private*. By declaring a member function explicitly, you prevent the compiler from generating its own version, and by making the function private, you keep people from calling it.

However, the scheme isn't foolproof: member and friend functions can still call your private function. *Unless*, that is, you are clever enough not to *define* the function. Then if you inadvertently call the function, you'll get an error at link-time (see Item 46).

For the `Array` class, then, your class declaration would start out like this:

```
class Array {
private:
  // Don't define this function!
  Array& operator=(const Array& rhs);

  ...

};
```

Now if a client tries to perform assignments on `Array` objects, the compiler will thwart the attempt, and if you inadvertently try it in a member or a friend function, the linker will yelp. This same little trick, by the way, is typically used in `iostream` library implementations to keep people from passing streams by value: the copy constructor is declared private and has no definition.

28 Use structs to partition the global namespace.

The biggest problem with the global scope is that there's only one of them. In a large software project, there is usually a great bevy of people putting names in this singular scope, and invariably this leads to name conflicts. For example, `library1.h` might define a number of constants, including the following:

```
const float LIB_VERSION = 1.204;
```

Ditto for `library2.h`:

```
const LIB_VERSION = 3;
```

It doesn't take great insight to see that there is going to be a problem if a program tries to include both `library1.h` and `library2.h`. Unfortunately, outside of cursing under your breath, sending hate mail to the library authors, and editing the header files until the name conflicts are eliminated, there is little you can do about this kind of problem.

You can, however, take pity on the poor souls who'll have your libraries foisted on them. By creating a struct to hold your global names, and by putting your global names inside this struct as static members, you can all but guarantee that your clients won't have to worry about name conflicts in the global scope.

```
struct MY_GLOBALS {
  // a library-global type
  enum Boolean { FALSE, TRUE };

  // a library-global function
  static Boolean licenseHasExpired();

  // a library-global object
  static const float LIB_VERSION;

  ...

};

// As usual, static data members must be
// initialized outside the struct
const float MY_GLOBALS::LIB_VERSION = 1.6;
```

Of course, a class will work as well as a struct, but since the only purpose for the struct is to partition the global name space, and because you want all the names to be public, a struct seems a bit more suited to the application. (In case it has slipped your mind, the only difference between a class and a struct is that members of a class are private by default, and members of a struct are public by default.)

Now when people want to access your global names, they simply prefix them with the scope name:

```
MY_GLOBALS::Boolean b = MY_GLOBALS::TRUE;

MY_GLOBALS::Boolean oldLicense =
  MY_GLOBALS::licenseHasExpired();

cout << MY_GLOBALS::LIB_VERSION;
```

If somebody else has used globals with the same names as you chose, there's not a problem, because the competing names will be in a different scope.

However, if there are no name conflicts at the global level, clients of your library may find it cumbersome to use the fully qualified names. Fortunately, there is a way you can let them have their scopes and ignore them too.

For your type names, provide typedefs that remove the need for explicit scoping. That is, for a type name T in your namespace struct G, provide a (global) typedef such that T is a synonym for G::T:

```
typedef MY_GLOBALS::Boolean Boolean;
```

For each (static) object X in your struct, provide a (global) reference X that is initialized with G::X:

```
const float& LIB_VERSION = MY_GLOBALS::LIB_VERSION;
```

You need to ensure that these objects are initialized before they're used. Consult Item 47 for all the ins and outs of how to do it.

Functions are treated just like objects, but the old use-a-global-reference trick is much more impressive when applied to functions in your struct, because who's ever heard of references to functions? Try to act casual when you show your colleagues this little number:

```
// make licenseHasExpired another name for
// MY_GLOBALS::licenseHasExpired; also impress your friends
MY_GLOBALS::Boolean (&licenseHasExpired)() =
  MY_GLOBALS::licenseHasExpired;
```

Given these typedefs and references, clients not suffering from global name conflicts can just use the unqualified type and object names, while clients who do have conflicts can simply ignore the typedef and reference declarations and use the fully qualified names. Because not all the clients of your library will want to use the shorthand names, you should be sure to put the typedefs and references in a different header file than the one containing your struct.

The only fly in the ointment is enumerator values, which must still be fully qualified. Even with the typedef, clients must still write

```
Boolean b = MY_GLOBALS::FALSE;
```

This is unfortunate, and the only way around it is to write macros for the enumerators:

```
#define FALSE MY_GLOBALS::FALSE
#define TRUE MY_GLOBALS::TRUE

Boolean b = FALSE;                 // use typedef and macro
```

This is a nice scheme, and everything (except enumerator values) is above board and fully supported by the language, but some party-pooper is sure to point out that references are virtually always implemented as pointers, so accessing members of your struct through the nicely named references is likely to cost one indirection per access. Needless to say, there are applications that can't afford such luxuries, although the number of programmers who are convinced they are working on such applications probably far outnumbers the applications where it's honestly an issue. Still, to shut them up (the programmers, not the applications), you (or they) can always fall back on the preprocessor:

```
#define LIB_VERSION MY_GLOBALS::LIB_VERSION
```

Classes and Functions: Implementation

Because C++ is strongly typed, coming up with appropriate declarations for your classes and functions is the lion's share of the battle. Given an appropriate declaration, it's hard to go wrong with the implementation. Yet, somehow, people manage to do it.

Some problems arise from inadvertently violating abstraction: accidentally allowing implementation details to peek out from behind the class and function boundaries that are supposed to contain them. Others originate in confusion over the length of an object's lifetime. Still others stem from premature optimization, typically traceable to the seductive nature of the `inline` keyword. Finally, some implementation strategies, while fine on a local scale, result in levels of coupling between source files that can make it unacceptably costly to recompile and/or relink larger programs.

Each of these problems, as well as others like them, can be avoided if you know what to watch out for. The items that follow identify some situations in which you need to be especially vigilant.

29 Avoid returning "handles" to internal data from `const` member functions.

A scene from an object-oriented romance:

> Object A: Darling, don't ever change!
>
> Object B: Don't worry, dear, I'm `const`.

Yet just as in real life, A wonders, "Can B be trusted?" And just as in real life, the answer often hinges on B's nature: the constitution of its member functions.

Suppose B is a constant `String` object:

```
class String {
private:
  char *data;

public:                                      •
  String(const char *value = 0);

  operator char *() const;        // convert String -> char*

  ...

};
  const String B("Hello World"); // B is a const object
```

Because B is const, it had better be the case that the value of B now and evermore is "Hello World". Of course, this supposes that programmers working with B are playing the game in a civilized fashion. In particular, it depends on the fact that nobody is "casting away the constness" of B through nefarious ploys such as this (see Item 21):

```
String& alsoB = (String&) B;   // make alsoB another name
                               // for B, but without the
                               // constness
```

Given that no one is doing such evil deeds, however, it seems a safe bet that B will never change. Or does it? Consider this sequence of events:

```
char *str = B;                 // calls B.operator char*

strcpy(str, "Hi Mom");         // modifies what str
                               // points to
```

Does B still have the value "Hello World", or has it suddenly mutated into a mother's greeting? The answer depends entirely on the implementation of String::operator char*.

Here's a careless implementation, one that does the wrong thing. However, it does it very efficiently, which is why so many programmers fall into this trap:

```
// a fast, but incorrect implementation
inline String::operator char*() const
{ return data; }
```

The flaw in this function is that it's returning a "handle" — in this case, a pointer — to the private field data of the String object on which the function is invoked. That handle gives callers unrestricted access to what data points to. In other words, after the statement

```
char *str = B;
```

the situation looks like this:

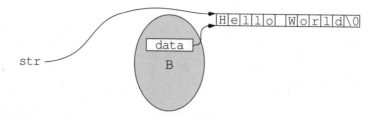

Clearly, any modification to the memory pointed to by str will also change the effective value of B. Thus, even though B is declared const, and even though only const member functions are invoked on B, B might still acquire different values as the program runs. In particular, if str modifies what it points to, B will also change.

There's nothing inherently wrong with the way String::operator char* is written. What's troublesome is that it can be applied to constant objects. If the function weren't declared const, there would be no problem, because it couldn't be applied to objects like B.

Yet it seems perfectly reasonable to turn a String object, even a constant one, into its equivalent char*, so you'd like to keep this function const. If you want to do that, you must rewrite your implementation to avoid returning a handle to the object's internal data:

```
// a slower, but correct implementation
inline String::operator char*() const
{
  char *copy = new char [strlen(data) + 1];
  strcpy(copy, data);

  return copy;

}
```

This implementation is safe, because it returns a pointer to memory that contains a *copy* of the data to which the String object points; there is no way to change the value of the String object through the pointer returned by this function. As usual, such safety commands a price: this version of String::operator char* is slower than the simple version above, and callers of this function must remember to call delete on the pointer that's returned.

If you think this version of operator char* is too slow, or if the potential memory leak makes you nervous (as well it should), a slightly different tack is to return a *constant* pointer:

```
class String {
public:
    operator const char *() const;

  ...

};
inline String::operator const char*() const
{ return data; }
```

This function is both fast and safe, but it's not the same as the one you originally specified. Furthermore, the constant return value may restrict callers unnecessarily. For all the gory details, see Item 21.

A pointer isn't the only way to return a handle to internal data; references are just as easy to abuse. Here's a common way to do it, again using the String class:

```
class String {
private:
  char *data;

public:
  String(const char *value = 0);

  char& operator[](int index) const
  { return data[index]; }

  ...

};
String string = "I'm not constant";

string[0] = 'x';                  // fine, string isn't const

const String constString = "I'm constant";

constString[0] = 'x';             // this modifies the const
                                  // string, but the compiler
                                  // won't notice
```

Notice how String::operator[] returns its result by reference. That means that the caller of this function gets back *another name* for the internal element data[index], and that other name can be used to modify the internal data of the supposedly constant object. This is the same problem as you saw before, but this time the culprit is a reference as a return value, not a pointer. The general solutions to this kind of problem are the same as they were for pointers: either make the function non-const, or rewrite it so that no handle is returned. For a solution to this *particular* problem — how to write String::operator[] so that it works for both const and non-const objects — see Item 21.

30 Avoid member functions that return pointers or references to members less accessible than themselves.

The reason for making a member private or protected is to limit access to it, right? Your overworked, underpaid C++ compiler goes to lots of trouble to make sure that your access restrictions aren't circumvented, right? So it doesn't make a lot of sense for you to write functions that give random clients the ability to freely access restricted members, now, does it? If you think it *does* make sense, please reread this paragraph over and over until you agree that it doesn't.

It's easy to violate this simple rule. Here's an example:

```
class String { ... };          // character strings

class Address { ... };         // where someone lives

class PhoneNumber { ... };

class Person {
protected:
  String name;
  Address address;
  PhoneNumber voiceNumber;
  PhoneNumber faxNumber;

public:
  Address& personAddress() { return address; }

  ...

};
```

The member function personAddress simply provides the caller with the Address object contained in the Person object, but, probably due to efficiency considerations, the result is returned by reference instead of by value (see Item 22). Unfortunately, the presence of this member function completely defeats the purpose of making Person::address protected:

```
Person scott(...);             // parameters omitted for
                               // simplicity

Address& addr =                // assume that addr is
  scott.personAddress();       // global
```

Notice that now the global object addr is *another name* for scott.address, and it can be used to read and write scott.address at will. For all practical purposes, scott.address is no longer protected; it is effectively public, and the source of this promotion in accessibility is the member function personAddress. Of course, there is nothing special about the access level `protected` in this example; if `address` were private, exactly the same reasoning would apply.

References aren't the only cause for concern; pointers can play this game, too. Here's the same example, but using pointers this time:

```
class Person {
protected:
  String name;
  Address address;
  PhoneNumber voiceNumber;
  PhoneNumber faxNumber;

public:
  Address * personAddress() { return &address; }

  ...

};

Address *addrPtr =
  scott.personAddress();        // same problem as above
```

With pointers, however, you have to worry not only about data members, but also about member *functions*. That's because it's possible to return a pointer to a member function:

```
class Person;                        // forward declaration for
                                     // typedef

// ppmf = "pointer to Person member function"
typedef void (Person::*ppmf)();

class Person {
protected:
  ...                                // same as above

  void verifyAddress();
public:
  static ppmf verificationFunction()
  { return &Person::verifyAddress; }

  ...

};
```

If you're not used to socializing with pointers to member functions and typedefs thereof, the declaration for `Person::verificationFunc-tion` may seem rather daunting. Don't be intimidated. All it says is

- `verificationFunction` is a member function taking no parameters;
- its return value is a pointer to a member function of the `Person` class;

- the pointed-to function (i.e., verificationFunction's return value) takes no parameters, and returns void.

As for the word static, that means what it always means in a member declaration: there is only one copy of the member for the entire class, and the member can be accessed without an object. For the complete story, consult your favorite introductory C++ textbook. (If your favorite introductory C++ textbook doesn't discuss static members, carefully tear out all its pages and recycle them. Dispose of the book's cover in an environmentally sound manner, and then borrow or buy a better textbook.)

In this last example, verifyAddress is a protected member function, indicating that it's really an implementation detail of the class; only class members and derived class members should know about it (and friends, too, of course). However, the public member function verificationFunction returns a pointer to verifyAddress, so clients can again pull this kind of thing:

```
ppmf pmf = scott.verificationFunction();

(scott.*pmf)();                    // same as calling
                                   // scott.verifyAddress
```

Here, pmf has become a synonym for Person::verifyAddress, with the crucial difference that there are no restrictions on its use.

In spite of the foregoing discussion, you may someday be faced with a situation in which, pressed to achieve performance constraints, you honestly need to write a member function that returns a reference or a pointer to a less-accessible member. At the same time, however, you won't want to sacrifice the access restrictions that private and protected afford you. In those cases, you can almost always achieve both goals by returning a pointer to or a reference to a const object. For details, take a look at Item 21.

31 Never return a reference to a local object or a dereferenced pointer initialized by new within the function.

This item may sound complicated, but it's not; it's simple common sense. Really. Honest. *Trust me.*

Consider first the matter of returning a reference to a local object. The problem here is that local objects are just that, *local*. That means that they're constructed when they're defined, and they're destructed when they go out of scope. Their scope, however, is that of the function body in which they're located. When the function returns, control leaves its scope, so the objects local to that function are automatically de-structed. As a result, if you return a reference to a local object, that local object has been destructed before the caller of the function ever gets its computational hands on it.

This problem usually raises its ugly head when you try to improve the efficiency of a function by returning its result by reference instead of by value. The following example is the same as the one in Item 23, which pursues in detail the question of when you can return a refer-ence and when you can't.

```
class Complex {                    // class for complex numbers
private:
  double r, i;                     // real, imaginary parts
                                   // of number

public:
  Complex(double realPart = 0, double imagPart = 0);
  ~Complex();

// notice that operator+ (incorrectly) returns a reference
friend Complex& operator+(const Complex& n1,
                          const Complex& n2);
};

// an incorrect implementation of operator+
inline Complex& operator+(const Complex& n1,
                          const Complex& n2)
{
  // create local object
  Complex result(n1.r + n2.r, n1.i + n2.i);

  // return reference to local object
  return result;
}
```

Here, the local object `result` is constructed upon entry into the body of `operator+`. Local objects have storage class `auto`, though, and `auto` objects have destructors automatically called on them when they go out of scope. The local object `result` will go out of scope after exe-cution of the `return` statement, so when you write this,

```
Complex two = 2;

Complex four = two + two;        // same as
                                 // operator+(two, two)
```

what happens during the function call is this:

1. The local object `result` is constructed.

2. A temporary reference is initialized to be another name for result, and this reference is squirreled away as operator+'s return value.

3. The local object result is destructed.

4. The object four is initialized using the temporary reference of
   step 2.

Everything is fine up until step 4, at which point there occurs, as they
say in the highest of high-tech circles, "a major lossage." The temporary reference initialized in step 2 ceased to refer to a valid object as of
the end of step 3, so the outcome of the initialization of object four is
completely undefined.

The lesson should be clear: don't return a reference to a local object.

"Okay," you say, "the problem is that the object I want to use goes out
of scope too soon. I can fix that. I'll just call new instead of using a local
object." Like this:

```
// another incorrect implementation of operator+
inline Complex& operator+(const Complex& n1,
                          const Complex& n2)
{
  // create a new object on the heap
  Complex *resultPtr =
    new Complex(n1.r + n2.r, n1.i + n2.i);

  // return it
  return *resultPtr;
}
```

This approach does indeed avoid the problem of the previous example,
but it introduces a new one in its place. In order to avoid a memory
leak in your software, you know that you must ensure that delete is
called on every pointer conjured up by new, but ay, there's the rub:
who's to make the matching call to delete for this function's call to
new?

Clearly, the *caller* of operator+ must see to it that the call to delete
is made. Clear, yes, and even easy to document, but nonetheless the
cause is hopeless. There are two reasons for this pessimistic assess-
ment.

First, it is a well-known fact that programmers, as a breed, are sloppy.
That doesn't mean that you're sloppy or that I'm sloppy, but rare is the
programmer who doesn't work with someone who is, shall we say, a little on the flaky side. What are the odds that such programmers — and
we all know they exist — will remember that whenever they call oper-

ator+, they must *take the address of the result* and then call `delete` on it? That is, they must use `operator+` like this:

```
Complex& four = two + two;        // get dereferenced pointer

...

delete &four;                     // retrieve pointer and
                                  // delete it
```

The odds are vanishingly small. Remember, if only a *single caller* of operator+ fails to follow the rules, you have a memory leak.

Returning dereferenced pointers has a second problem, a more serious one, because it persists even in the presence of the most conscientious of programmers. Often, the result of operator+ is a temporary intermediate value, an object that exists only for the purposes of evaluating a larger expression. For example:

```
Complex one(1), two(2), three(3), four(4);
Complex sum;

sum = one + two + three + four;
```

Evaluation of the expression to be assigned to `sum` requires three separate calls to `operator+`, a fact that becomes quite evident when you rewrite the expression in its completely equivalent functional form:

```
sum = operator+(operator+(operator+(one, two), three), four);
```

You know that each of the calls to `operator+` returns an object that needs to be deleted, but there is no possibility of calling `delete`, because none of the returned objects has been saved anywhere.

The only solution to this difficulty is to ask clients to code like this:

```
Complex& temp1 = one + two;
Complex& temp2 = temp1 + three;
Complex& temp3 = temp2 + four;

delete &temp1;
delete &temp2;
delete &temp3;
```

Do that, and the best you can hope for is that people will ignore you. More realistically, you'd be skinned alive, or possibly sentenced to ten years hard labor writing microcode for waffle irons and toaster ovens.

Learn your lesson now, then: writing a function that returns a dereferenced pointer is a memory leak just waiting to happen.

32 Use enums for integral class constants.

Being a fervent disciple of the school of abstraction, you find the following class an offense to your very being:

```
class X {
  char buffer[100];
};
```

In particular, you object to the literal 100 — a symbolic name would be so much better. You rewrite the code thusly:

```
const BUFSIZE = 100;                 // see Item 1

class X {
  char buffer[BUFSIZE];
};
```

You then sleep soundly until you encounter this in the same program:

```
class Y {
  int buffer[256];
};
```

You're about to pull the same trick with Y that you pulled with X when your training in the ways of encapsulation kicks in, and it occurs to you that the names of class-specific symbolic constants should really be local to the class in which they're used. You'd like to do something like this,

```
class X {
  static const BUFSIZE = 100;   // error!
  char buffer[BUFSIZE];
};
```

but static members can't be defined in the class definition, they can only be declared. Unfortunately, if you move the initialization outside the class definition, the compiler no longer knows the value of BUFSIZE at the point where it needs to allocate space for the buffers:

```
class X {
  static const BUFSIZE;
  char buffer[BUFSIZE];          // error!
};

const X::BUFSIZE = 100;
```

The solution to your dilemma is to take advantage of the fact that an enum is a symbolic name for an int, and an enum can be given a value at the point of declaration. Hence:

```
class X {
  enum { BUFSIZE = 100 };        // fine
  char buffer[BUFSIZE];          // fine
};
```

Some people find this to be a grotesque hack, others find it to be a testimonial to the elegance of the language, but everybody agrees on one thing: it works. And that counts for something. Be forewarned, however, that the representation for an enumerator need not be any larger than that for an int, so whatever values your class constants are to take on, they had better be within the range of an int.

33 Use inlining judiciously.

Inline functions — what a *wonderful* idea! They look like functions, they act like functions, they're ever so much better than macros (see Item 1), and you can call them without having to incur the overhead of a function call. What more could you possibly ask for?

You actually get more than you might think, because avoiding the cost of a function call is only half the story. Optimizing compilers — still a relative rarity in the C++ world, but not for *too* much longer, we hope — are typically designed to concentrate on stretches of code that lack function calls, so when you inline a function, you may enable the compiler to perform context-specific optimizations on the body of the function. Such optimizations would be impossible for "normal" function calls. Even if you don't have access to an optimizing compiler now, you may start using one later, so judicious inlining now might well yield unanticipated benefits in the future. Wouldn't that be a pleasant surprise?

However, let's not get carried away. In programming, as in life, there is no free lunch, and inline functions are no exception. The whole idea behind an inline function is to replace each call of that function with its code body, and it doesn't take a Ph.D. in statistics to see that this is likely to increase the overall size of your object code. On machines with limited memory, then, overzealous inlining can give rise to programs that are too big for the available memory. On machines with virtual memory, inline-induced code bloat can lead to pathological paging behavior (thrashing) that will slow your program to a crawl. It will, however, provide your disk controller with a nice exercise regimen.

On the other hand, if an inline function body is *very* short, the code generated for the function body may actually be smaller than the code generated for a function call. If that is the case, inlining the function may actually lead to *smaller* object code!

Bear in mind that the `inline` directive is a *hint* to the compiler, not a command (just like `register`). That means the compiler is free to ignore your inline directive whenever it wants to, and it's not that hard to make it want to. For example, most compilers refuse to inline functions that are recursive, and many of them won't inline complicated functions, either. In fact, one popular C++ compiler stops inlining when the "inline complexity measure" of a function exceeds 20. Twenty? Nobody seems to know what the mystical significance of that 20 is (it used to be 12 in an earlier release of the compiler), much less the units in which it is measured, but deep down in the bowels of the compiler is encoded the injunction, "Thou shalt not inline functions more complicated than 20." And that compiler doesn't.

Needless to say, a different compiler might be more daring. Or less daring. That means that whether a given inline function is actually inlined is inherently dependent on the implementation of the compiler you're using. However, most compilers will issue a warning (see Item 48) if they fail to inline a function you've asked them to.

Suppose you've written some function `f` and you've declared it `inline`. What happens if the compiler chooses, for whatever reason, not to inline that function? The obvious answer is that `f` will be treated like a non-inline function: code for `f` will be generated as if it were a "normal" function, and calls to `f` will proceed as "normal" function calls.

Unfortunately, the obvious answer is not quite right. Think about it for a minute, and you'll realize that inline function definitions are virtually always put in header files. This allows multiple translation units (source files) to include the same header files and reap the advantages of the inline functions that are defined within them. Here's an example, in which I adopt the convention that source files end in ".cc", one of a variety of incompatible file naming conventions currently competing for favor in the world of C++:

```
// This is file example.h
inline void f() { ... }        // definition of f

...


// This is file source1.cc
#include "example.h"            // includes definition of f

...
```

```
// This is file source2.cc
#include "example.h"          // also includes definition
                             // of f
 ...
```

Under the assumption that f is *not* being inlined, when source1.cc is compiled, the resulting object file will contain a function called f. Similarly, when source2.cc is compiled, its generated object file will also contain a function called f. When you try to link the two object files together, then, your linker will complain that your program contains two definitions of f, an error.

To prevent just this problem, compilers treat an inline function that they aren't inlining as if the function had been declared static — that is, local to the file currently being compiled. In the example you just saw, the compiler would treat f as if it were static in source1.cc when that file was being compiled, and as if it were static in source2.cc when that file was being compiled. This strategy eliminates the link-time problem, but at a cost: each translation unit that includes the definition of f will have its own static copy of f.

This leads to a stunning realization. If an inline function isn't inlined, you *still* pay for the cost of a function call at each call site, but you *also* suffer an increase in code size, because each translation unit that includes f's definition gets its own copy of f's code!

There's more. Sometimes your poor, embattled compiler has to generate a function body for an inline function even when the compiler is perfectly willing to inline the function. In particular, if your program ever takes the address of an inline function, the compiler must generate a function body for it; how can it come up with a pointer to a function that doesn't exist?

```
inline void f() {...}        // as above

void (*pf)() = f;            // pf points to f

main()
{
  f();                       // an inline call to f

  pf();                      // a non-inline call to f
                             // through pf
}
```

In this case, you end up in the seemingly paradoxical situation whereby calls to f are inlined, but each translation unit that takes f's address still generates a static copy of the function. Fortunately, such situations are rare.

For purposes of program development, it is of course important to keep the above considerations in mind, but from a purely practical point of view during coding, one fact dominates all others: most debuggers cannot cope with inline functions.

This shouldn't be surprising. How do you set a breakpoint in a function that isn't there? How do you step through such a function? How do you trap calls to it? Without being unreasonably clever (or deviously underhanded), you simply can't do it. Happily, this leads to a logical strategy for determining which functions should be declared `inline` and which should not.

Initially, don't inline anything, or at least limit your inlining to those functions that are truly trivial, such as `age` below:

```
class Person {
private:
  unsigned short personAge;

  ...

public:
  unsigned short age() const { return personAge; }

  ...

};
```

By employing inlines cautiously, you facilitate your use of a debugger, but you also put inlining in its proper place: as a hand-applied optimization. Don't forget the empirically determined rule of 80-20, which states that a typical program spends 80 percent of its time executing only 20 percent of its code. It's an important rule, because it reminds you that your goal as a software developer is to identify the 20 percent of your code that is actually capable of increasing your program's overall performance. You can inline and otherwise tweak your functions until the cows come home, but it's all wasted effort unless you're focusing on the *right* functions.

Once you've identified the set of important functions in your application, the ones whose inlining will actually make a difference (a set that is itself dependent on the architecture on which you're running), don't hesitate to declare them `inline`. At the same time, however, be on the lookout for problems caused by code bloat, and watch out for compiler warnings (see Item 48) that indicate that your inline functions haven't been inlined.

Used judiciously, inline functions are an invaluable component of every C++ programmer's toolbox, but, as the foregoing discussion has revealed, they're not quite as simple and straightforward as you might have thought.

34 Minimize compilation dependencies between files.

So you go into your C++ program and you make a minor change to the implementation of a class. Not the class interface, mind you, just the implementation; only the private stuff. Then you get set to rebuild the program, figuring that the compilation and linking should take only a few seconds. After all, only one class has been modified. You type make (or its moral equivalent), and you are astonished, then mortified, as you realize that the whole *world* is being recompiled and relinked!

Don't you just *hate* it when that happens?

The problem is that C++ doesn't do a very good job of separating interfaces from implementations. In particular, class declarations include not only the interface specification (typically in the public and protected sections), but also the implementation details. For example:

```
class Person {
private:
  String name_;                 // implementation detail
  Date birthDate_;              // implementation detail
  Address address_;             // implementation detail
  Country citizenship_;         // implementation detail

public:
  Person(const String& name, const Date& birthday,
         const Address& addr, const Country& country);
  virtual ~Person();

  const char * name() const;
  const char * birthDate () const;
  const char * address() const;
  const char * nationality() const;
};
```

This is hardly a Nobel prize-winning class design, although it does illustrate an interesting naming convention for distinguishing private data from public functions when the same name makes sense for both: the former are tagged with a trailing underbar. The important thing to observe is that class Person can't be compiled unless the compiler also has access to declarations for the classes in terms of which Person is implemented, namely, String, Date, Address, and Country. Such declarations are typically provided through #include directives, so at the top of the file containing the Person class declaration, you are likely to find something like this:

```
#include "string.h"
#include "date.h"
#include "address.h"
#include "country.h"
```

Unfortunately, this sets up a compilation dependency between the file containing the Person class declaration and these additional files. As a result, if any of these auxiliary classes changes its implementation, or if any of the classes on which the auxiliary class depends changes *its* implementation, then the file containing the Person class must be recompiled, as must any files that use the Person class. For clients of the Person class, this is more than annoying, it can be downright painful.

You might wonder why C++ insists on putting the implementation details of a class in the class declaration. For example, why can't you declare the Person class like this,

```
class String;              // forward declaration
class Date;                // forward declaration
class Address;             // forward declaration
class Country;             // forward declaration

class Person {
public:
  Person(const String& name, const Date& birthday,
         const Address& addr, const Country& country);
  virtual ~Person();

  const char * name() const;
  const char * birthDate () const;
  const char * address() const;
  const char * nationality() const;
};
```

specifying the implementation details of the class separately? If that were possible, clients of Person would have to be recompiled only if the interface to the class changed. Because interfaces tend to stabilize long before implementations do, such a separation of interface from implementation could save untold hours of recompilation and linking over the course of a large software effort.

Unfortunately, the real world intrudes on this idyllic scenario, as you will appreciate when you consider something like this:

```
main()
{
  int x;                    // declare/define an int

  Person p(...);            // declare/define a Person
                            // (arguments omitted for
                            // simplicity)

  ...

}
```

When the compiler sees the declaration for x, it knows that it must allocate enough space to hold an int. No problem, it knows how big an int is. When the compiler sees the declaration for p, however, it knows that it has to allocate enough space for a Person, but how is it supposed to know how big a Person object is? The only way it can get that information is to consult the class declaration, but if it were legal for a class declaration to omit the implementation details, how would the compiler know how much space to allocate?

In principle, this is in no way an insuperable problem — languages such as Smalltalk, Eiffel, and Objective C get around it all the time. The way they do it is by allocating only enough space for a *pointer* to an object when an object is declared. That is, they handle the code above as if it had been written like this:

```
main()
{
  int x;                    // declare/define an int

  Person *p;                // declare/define a pointer
                            // to a Person
  ...

}
```

It may have occurred to you that this is in fact legal C++, and it turns out that you can play the "hide the object implementation behind a pointer" game yourself.

Here's how you employ the technique to decouple Person's interface from its implementation. First, you put only the following in the header file declaring the Person class:

```
// the compiler still needs to know about these class
// names for the Person constructor
class String;
class Date;
class Address;
class Country;

// class PersonImpl will contain the implementation
// details of a Person object; this is just a
// forward declaration of the class name
class PersonImpl;

class Person {
private:
  PersonImpl *impl;              // pointer to implementation
```

```
public:
  Person(const String& name, const Date& birthday,
         const Address& addr, const Country& country);
  virtual ~Person();

  const char * name() const;
  const char * birthDate () const;
  const char * address() const;
  const char * nationality() const;
};
```

Now clients of `Person` are completely divorced from the details of strings, dates, addresses, countries, and persons. Those classes can be modified at will, but clients of `Person` may remain blissfully unaware. More to the point, they may remain blissfully un-recompiled. This is a true separation of interface and implementation.

Classes like `Person` that contain only a pointer to an unspecified implementation are sometimes called *Handle* classes or, more poetically, *Cheshire Cat* classes.

A different approach is to make `Person` an *Abstract Base Class* (ABC), sometimes called a *Protocol class*. By definition, an ABC has no implementation; its *raison d'être* is to specify an interface for derived classes (see Item 36). As a result, it typically has no data members, no constructors, a virtual destructor (see Item 14), and a set of pure virtual functions that specify the interface. An ABC for `Person` might look like this:

```
class Person {
public:
  virtual ~Person();

  virtual const char * name() const = 0;
  virtual const char * birthDate () const = 0;
  virtual const char * address() const = 0;
  virtual const char * nationality() const = 0;
};
```

Clients of the `Person` class program in terms of `Person` pointers and references, since it's not possible to instantiate classes containing pure virtual functions. Like clients of Handle classes, clients of ABCs need no recompilation if only the implementation of the ABC changes.

Of course, clients of an ABC must have *some* way of creating new objects. They do it by instantiating concrete classes derived from the ABC. For example, the `Person` class might have a derived class `Real-Person` that can be instantiated:

```
class RealPerson: public Person {
private:
  PersonImpl impl;                    // implementation object

public:
  RealPerson(const String& name, const Date& birthday,
             const Address& addr, const Country& country)
  : impl(name, birthday, addr, country) {}

  virtual ~RealPerson() {}

  const char * name() const
  { return impl.name(); }

  const char * birthDate () const
  { return impl.birthDate(); }

  const char * address() const
  { return impl.address(); }

  const char * nationality() const
  { return impl.nationality(); }
};
```

RealPerson demonstrates one of the two most common mechanisms for implementing an ABC: it inherits from the ABC (Person), and it contains an object that actually implements the ABC's functionality. RealPerson itself does no more than map function interfaces inherited from the ABC into function implementations offered by the underlying implementation object. Characteristically, each of RealPerson's functions is trivial.

The second common way to implement an ABC involves multiple inheritance, a topic explored in Item 43.

Okay, so Handle classes and ABCs decouple interfaces from implementations, thereby reducing compilation dependencies between files. Cynic that you are, I know you're waiting for the fine print. "What does all this hocus-pocus cost me?," you mutter. The answer is the usual one in computer science: it costs you some speed at runtime, plus some additional memory per object.

In the case of Handle classes, any member function that accesses part of the implementation — that's all of them, for all practical purposes — has to go through the implementation pointer. That adds one level of indirection per access. In addition, you must add the size of this implementation pointer to the amount of memory required to store each object.

For ABCs, every function call is virtual, so you pay the cost of an indirect jump each time you make a function call (see Item 14). Also, objects derived from the ABC must contain a virtual pointer (again, see

Item 14), which, depending on whether the ABC is the exclusive source of virtual functions for the objects, may increase the amount of memory needed to store an object.

Finally, neither Handle classes nor ABCs can get much use out of inline functions. All practical uses of inlines require access to implementation details, and that's the very thing that Handle classes and ABCs were designed to avoid in the first place.

It would be a serious mistake, however, to dismiss Handle classes and ABCs simply because they have a cost associated with them. So do virtual functions, and you wouldn't want to forgo those, would you? (If so, you're reading the wrong book.) Instead, consider using these techniques in an evolutionary manner: use Handle classes and ABCs during development to minimize the impact on clients when implementations change; replace Handle classes and ABCs with concrete classes for production use when it can be shown that the difference in speed and/or size is significant enough to justify the increased coupling between classes. Someday in the not-too-distant future, tools will be available to perform this kind of transformation for you automatically.

A skillful blending of Handle classes, ABCs, and concrete classes will allow you to develop software systems that are efficient to execute as well as easy to evolve, but there is a serious disadvantage: you may have to cut down on the long breaks you've been taking while your programs have been recompiling.

Inheritance and
Object-Oriented Design

Many people are of the opinion that inheritance is what object-oriented programming is all about. Whether that's so is currently a point of considerable contention, but the number of items in the other sections of this book should convince you that as far as effective C++ programming is concerned, you have a lot more tools at your disposal than simply specifying which classes inherit from which other classes.

Still, designing and implementing class hierarchies is fundamentally different from anything found in the world of C; certainly it is in the area of inheritance and object-oriented design that you are most likely to radically rethink your approach to the construction of software systems. Furthermore, C++ provides a bewildering assortment of object-oriented building blocks, including public, protected, and private base classes; virtual and nonvirtual base classes; and virtual and nonvirtual member functions. Each of these features interacts not only with one another, but also with the other components of the language. As a result, trying to understand what each feature means, when it should be used, and how it is best combined with the non-object-oriented aspects of C++ is an arduous and daunting endeavor.

Further complicating the matter is the fact that different features of the language appear to do more or less the same thing. Examples:

- You need a collection of classes with many shared characteristics. Should you use inheritance and have all the classes derived from a common base class, or should you use templates and have them all generated from a common code skeleton?

- Class A is to be implemented in terms of class B. Should A have a data member of type B, or should A privately inherit from B?

- You need to design a type-safe homogeneous container class, such as a set, a list, a queue, a heap, a binary tree, etc. Should you use templates, or would it be better to build type-safe interfaces around a class that is itself implemented using generic (void*) pointers?

In the items in this section, I offer guidance on how to answer questions such as these. However, I cannot hope to address every aspect of object-oriented design. Entire books have been written on the topic, and still there is much that is only poorly understood. Instead, I concentrate on explaining what the different features in C++ really *mean*, on what you are really *saying* when you use a particular feature. For example, public inheritance means "isa" (see Item 35), and if you try to make it mean anything else, you will run into trouble. Similarly, a virtual function means "interface must be inherited," while a nonvirtual function means "both interface *and* implementation must be inherited." Failing to distinguish between these meanings has caused many a C++ programmer untold grief.

If you understand the meanings of C++'s varied features, you'll find that your outlook on object-oriented design shifts. Instead of it being an exercise in differentiating between language constructs, it will properly become a matter of figuring out what it is you want to say about your software system. Once you know what you want to say, you'll be able to translate that into the appropriate C++ features without too much difficulty.

The importance of saying what you mean and understanding what you're saying cannot be overestimated. The items that follow provide a detailed examination of how to do this effectively, and Item 44 summarizes the correspondence between C++'s object-oriented constructs and what they mean. It serves as a nice capstone for this section, as well as a concise reference for future consultation.

35 Make sure public inheritance models "isa."

In his book, *Some Must Watch While Some Must Sleep* (W. H. Freeman and Company, 1974), William Dement relates the story of his attempt to fix in the minds of his students the most important lessons of his course. It is claimed, he said to his class, that the average British schoolchild remembers little more history than that the Battle of Hastings was in 1066. If a child remembers little else, Dement emphasized, he or she remembers the date 1066. For the students in *his* course, Dement went on, there were only a few central messages, including, interestingly enough, the fact that sleeping pills cause insomnia. He implored his students to remember these few critical facts even if they forgot everything else discussed in the course, and he returned to these fundamental precepts repeatedly during the term.

At the end of the course, the last question on the final exam was, "Write one thing from the course that you will surely remember for the rest of your life." When Dement graded the exams, he was stunned. Nearly everyone had written, "1066."

It is thus with great trepidation that I proclaim to you now that the single most important rule in object-oriented programming with C++ is this: public inheritance means "isa." Commit this rule to memory.

If you write that class D ("Derived") publicly inherits from class B ("Base"), you are telling the C++ compiler (as well as any human reader of your code) that every object of type D is also an object of type B, but *not vice-versa*. You are saying that anything that is true of an object of type B is also true of an object of type D, but *not vice-versa*. You are saying that B represents a more general concept than D, that D represents a more specialized concept than B. You are asserting that anywhere an object of type B can be used, an object of type D can be used just as well, because every object of type D *isa* object of type B. On the other hand, if you need an object of type D, an object of type B will not do: every D isa B, but not vice-versa.

C++ enforces this interpretation of public inheritance. Consider this example:

```
class Person { ... };
class Student: public Person { ... };
```

We know from everyday experience that every student is a person, but not every person is a student. That is exactly what this hierarchy asserts. We expect that anything that is true of a person, for example, that he or she has a date of birth, is also true of a student, but we do not expect that everything that is true of a student — that he or she is enrolled in a particular school, for instance — is true of people in general. The notion of a person is more general than is that of a student; a student is a specialized type of person.

Within the realm of C++, any function that expects an argument of type Person (or pointer-to-Person, or reference-to-Person) will take a Student object (or pointer-to-Student, or reference-to-Student) instead:

```
void dance(const Person& p);    // anyone can dance
void study(const Student& s);   // only students study

Person p;                       // p is a Person
Student s;                      // s is a Student
```

```
dance(p);                          // fine, p is a Person

dance(s);                          // fine, s is a Student,
                                   // and a Student isa Person

study(s);                          // fine

study(p);                          // error! p isn't a Student
```

This is true only for *public* inheritance. C++ will behave as I've just described only if Student is publicly derived from Person. Private inheritance means something entirely different (see Item 41), and no one seems to know what protected inheritance (a latecomer on the scene anyway) is supposed to mean.

The equivalence of public inheritance and isa sounds simple, but in practice things aren't always so straightforward. Sometimes your intuition can mislead you. For example, it is a fact that a penguin is a bird, and it is a fact that birds can fly. If we naively try to express this in C++, our effort yields:

```
class Bird {
public:
  virtual void fly();          // birds can fly

  ...

};

class Penguin: public Bird {    // penguins are birds
  ...
};
```

Suddenly we are in trouble, because this hierarchy says that penguins can fly, which we know not to be the case. What happened?

In this case, we are the victims of an imprecise language (English). When we say that birds can fly, we don't really mean that *all* birds can fly, only that, in general, birds have the ability to fly. If we were more precise, we'd recognize that there are in fact several types of non-flying birds, and we would come up with the following hierarchy, which models reality much better:

```
class Bird {

  ...                          // no fly function is
                               // declared

};

class FlyingBird: public Bird {
public:
  virtual void fly();

  ...
```

```
};

class NonFlyingBird: public Bird {
    ...                             // no fly function is
                                    // declared
};

class Penguin: public NonFlyingBird {
    ...                             // no fly function is
                                    // declared
};
```

This hierarchy is much more faithful to what we really know than was the original design.

Even now we're not entirely finished with penguins, because, in fact, for some software systems, it may be entirely appropriate to say that a penguin isa bird. In particular, if your application has much to do with beaks and wings and nothing whatsoever to do with flying, the original hierarchy might work out just fine. Irritating though this may seem, it's a simple reflection of the fact that there is no one ideal design for all software. The best design depends on what the system is expected to do, both now and in the future. If your application has no knowledge of flying, and isn't ever expected to have any, making Penguin a derived class of Bird may be a perfectly valid design decision. In fact, it may be preferable to a decision that makes a distinction between flying and non-flying birds, because such a distinction would be absent from the world you are trying to model. Adding superfluous classes to a hierarchy can be just as bad a design decision as having the wrong inheritance relationships between classes.

There is another school of thought on how to handle what I call the "All birds can fly, penguins are birds, penguins can't fly, uh oh" problem. That is to redefine the fly function for penguins so that it generates a runtime error:

```
void error(const char *msg);    // defined elsewhere

class Penguin: public Bird {
public:
  virtual void fly() { error("Penguins can't fly!"); }

  ...

};
```

Interpreted languages such as Smalltalk tend to adopt this approach, but it's important to recognize that this says something entirely different from what you might think. This does *not* say "Penguins can't fly"; this says, "Penguins can fly, but it's an error for them to try to do so."

How can you tell the difference? From the time at which the error message is issued. The injunction, "Penguins can't fly," can be enforced by the compiler, but violations of the statement, "It's an error for penguins to try to fly," can be detected only at runtime.

To express the constraint, "Penguins can't fly," you make sure that no such function is defined for Penguin objects:

```
class Bird {

    ...                           // no fly function is
                                  // declared
};

class NonFlyingBird: public Bird {

    ...                           // no fly function is
                                  // declared
};

class Penguin: public NonFlyingBird {

    ...                           // no fly function is
                                  // declared
};
```

If you try to make a penguin fly, the compiler will reprimand you for your transgression:

```
Penguin p;

p.fly();                          // error!
```

This is very different from the behavior you get if you use the Smalltalk approach, because with that methodology, the compiler won't say a word.

The C++ philosophy is fundamentally different from the Smalltalk philosophy, so you're better off doing things the C++ way as long as you're programming in C++. In addition, there are certain technical advantages to detecting errors at compile-time instead of at runtime — see Item 46.

Of course, the isa relationship is not the only one that can exist between classes. Two other common inter-class relationships are "has-a" and "is-implemented-in-terms-of." These relationships are considered in Items 40 and 41. It's not uncommon for C++ designs to go awry because one of these other important relationships was incorrectly modeled as isa, so you should make sure that you understand the differences between these fundamental relationships and that you know how they are best modeled in C++.

36 Differentiate between inheritance of interface and inheritance of implementation.

The seemingly straightforward notion of (public) inheritance turns out, upon closer examination, to actually be composed of two separable parts: inheritance of function interfaces and inheritance of function implementations. The difference between these two kinds of inheritance corresponds exactly to the difference between function declarations and function definitions discussed in the introduction to this book.

As a class designer, you sometimes want derived classes to inherit only the interface (declaration) of a member function; sometimes you want derived classes to inherit both the interface and the implementation for a function, but you want to allow them to override the implementation you provide; and sometimes you want them to inherit both interface and implementation without allowing them to override anything.

To get a better feel for the differences amongst these options, consider a class hierarchy for representing geometric shapes in a graphics application:

```
class Shape {
public:
  virtual void draw() const = 0;

  virtual void error(const char *msg);

  int objectID() const;

  ...

};

class Rectangle: public Shape { ... };

class Ellipse: public Shape { ... };
```

Shape is an abstract class — its pure virtual function draw marks it as such. As a result, clients cannot create instances of the Shape class, only of the classes derived from it. Nonetheless, Shape exerts a strong influence on all the classes that (publicly) inherit from it, because

- Member function *interfaces are always inherited.* As is explained in Item 35, public inheritance means isa, so anything that is true of a base class must also be true of its derived classes. Hence, if a function applies to a class, it must also apply to its subclasses.

Three functions are declared in the Shape class. The first, draw, draws the current object on an implicit display. The second, error, is called by member functions if they need to report an error. The third, objectID, returns a unique integer identifier for the current object;

Item 17 gives an example of how such a function might be used. Each function is declared in a different way: `draw` is a pure virtual function; `error` is a simple (impure?) virtual function; and `objectID` is a non-virtual function. What are the implications of these different declarations?

Consider first the pure virtual function `draw`. The two most salient features of pure virtual functions are that they *must* be redeclared by any non-abstract class that inherits them, and they typically have no definition in abstract classes. Put these two traits together, and you realize that

- The purpose of declaring a pure virtual function is to have derived classes inherit a function *interface only.*

This makes perfect sense for the `Shape::draw` function, because it is a reasonable demand that all `Shape` objects must be `drawable`, but the `Shape` class can provide no reasonable default implementation for that function — the algorithm for drawing an ellipse is very different than the algorithm for drawing a rectangle, for example. A good way to interpret the declaration of `Shape::draw` is as saying to designers of subclasses, "You have to provide a `draw` function, but I have no idea how you're going to implement it."

Incidentally, it *is* possible to provide a definition for a pure virtual function. That is, you could provide an implementation for `Shape::-draw`, and C++ wouldn't complain, but the only way to call it would be to fully specify the call with the class name:

```
Shape *ps = new Shape;          // error! Shape is abstract

Shape *ps1 = new Rectangle;     // fine
ps1->draw();                    // calls Rectangle::draw

Shape *ps2 = new Ellipse;       // fine
ps2->draw();                    // calls Ellipse::draw

ps1->Shape::draw();             // calls Shape::draw

ps2->Shape::draw();             // calls Shape::draw
```

This little-known feature of the language is generally of limited utility, but it can be used as a mechanism for providing a default implementation for simple (impure) virtual functions, as you'll see below.

Sometimes it's useful to declare a class containing *nothing* but pure virtual functions. Such an *Abstract Base Class* (ABC) can only provide function interfaces for derived classes, never implementations. ABCs are described in Item 34, and are mentioned again in Item 43.

The scoop on simple virtual functions is a bit different from that for pure virtuals. As usual, derived classes inherit the interface of the function, but simple virtual functions traditionally provide an implementation that derived classes may or may not choose to override. If you think about this for a minute, you'll realize that

- The purpose of declaring a simple virtual function is to have derived classes inherit a function *interface as well as a default implementation.*

In the case of `Shape::error`, the interface says that every class must support a function to be called when an error is encountered, but each class is free to handle errors in whatever way it sees fit. If a class doesn't want to do anything special, it can just fall back on the default error-handling provided in the `Shape` class. That is, the declaration of `Shape::error` says to designers of subclasses, "You've got to support an `error` function, but if you don't want to write your own, you can fall back on the default version in the `Shape` class."

It turns out that it can be dangerous to allow simple virtual functions to specify both a function declaration and a default implementation. For example, consider a hierarchy of airplanes for XYZ Airlines. XYZ has only two kinds of planes, the Model A and the Model B, and both are flown precisely the same way. Hence, XYZ designs the following hierarchy:

```
class Airport { ... };          // represents airports

class Airplane {
public:
  virtual void fly(const Airport& destination);

  ...

};

void Airplane::fly(const Airport& destination)
{
  default code for flying an airplane to
  the given destination
}

class ModelA: public Airplane { ... };

class ModelB: public Airplane { ... };
```

To express the fact that all planes have to support a `fly` function, and in recognition of the fact that different models of plane could, in principle, require different implementations for `fly`, `Airplane::fly` is declared virtual. However, in order to avoid writing identical code in the `ModelA` and `ModelB` classes, the default flying behavior is provided as the body of `Airplane::fly`, which both `ModelA` and `ModelB` inherit. So far, so good.

Now suppose that XYZ Airlines, its fortunes on the rise, decides to acquire a new type of airplane, the Model C. The Model C is quite dissimilar from the Model A and the Model B. In particular, it is flown completely differently.

XYZ's programmers add the class for Model C to the hierarchy, but in their haste to get the new model into service, they forget to redefine the fly function:

```
class ModelC: public Airplane {

    ...                             // no fly function is
                                    // declared

};
```

In their code, then, they have something akin to the following:

```
Airport JFK(...);

Airplane *pa = new ModelC;

...

pa->fly(JFK);                       // calls Airplane::fly!
```

This is a disaster: an attempt is being made to fly a `ModelC` object as if it were a `ModelA` or a `ModelB`. That's not the kind of behavior that inspires confidence in the traveling public.

The problem here is not that `Airplane::fly` has default behavior, but that `ModelC` was allowed to inherit that behavior without explicitly saying that it wanted to. Fortunately, it's easy to offer default behavior to subclasses, but not give it to them unless they ask for it. The trick is to sever the connection between the interface of the virtual function and its default implementation. Here's one way to do it:

```
class Airplane {
public:
  virtual void fly(const Airport& destination) = 0;

  ...

protected:
  void defaultFly(const Airport& destination);
};

void Airplane::defaultFly(const Airport& destination)
{
  default code for flying an airplane to
  the given destination
}
```

Notice how `Airplane::fly` has been turned into a *pure* virtual function. That provides the interface for flying. The default implementation is also present in the `Airplane` class, but now it's in the form of an independent function, `defaultFly`. Classes like `ModelA` and `ModelB` that want to use the default behavior simply make an inline call to `defaultFly` inside their body of `fly`:

```
class ModelA: public Airplane {
public:
  virtual void fly(const Airport& destination)
  { defaultFly(destination); }

  ...

};

class ModelB: public Airplane {
public:
  virtual void fly(const Airport& destination)
  { defaultFly(destination); }

  ...

};
```

For the `ModelC` class, however, there is no possibility of accidentally inheriting the incorrect implementation of `fly`, because the pure virtual in `Airplane` forces `ModelC` to provide its own version of `fly`.

```
class ModelC: public Airplane {
public:
  virtual void fly(const Airport& destination);

  ...

};

void ModelC::fly(const Airport& destination)
{
  code for flying a ModelC airplane to the given destination
}
```

This scheme isn't foolproof, but it's substantially more reliable than the original design.

As for `Airplane::defaultFly`, it's protected because it's truly an implementation detail of `Airplane` and its derived classes; clients using airplanes should care only that they can be flown, not how the flying is implemented.

It's also important that `Airplane::defaultFly` is a *nonvirtual* function. This is because no subclass should redefine this function, a topic treated later in this item, as well as in Item 37. If `defaultFly` were virtual, you'd have a circular problem: what if some subclass forgets to redefine `defaultFly` when it's supposed to?

Some people object to the idea of having separate functions for providing interface and default implementation, such as `fly` and `defaultFly` above. Yet they still agree that interface and default implementation should be separated. How do they resolve this seeming contradiction? By taking advantage of the fact that pure virtual functions must be redeclared in subclasses but may also have implementations of their own. Here's how the `Airplane` hierarchy could take advantage of the ability to define a pure virtual function:

```
class Airplane {
public:
  virtual void fly(const Airport& destination) = 0;

  ...

};

void Airplane::fly(const Airport& destination)
{
  default code for flying an airplane to
  the given destination
}

class ModelA: public Airplane {
public:
  virtual void fly(const Airport& destination)
  { Airplane::fly(destination); }

  ...

};

class ModelB: public Airplane {
public:
  virtual void fly(const Airport& destination)
  { Airplane::fly(destination); }

  ...

};

class ModelC: public Airplane {
public:
  virtual void fly(const Airport& destination);

  ...

};

void ModelC::fly(const Airport& destination)
{
  code for flying a ModelC airplane to the given destination
}
```

This is exactly the same design you had before, except that the body of the pure virtual function `Airplane::fly` takes the place of the independent function `Airplane::defaultFly`.

Finally, we come to `Shape`'s nonvirtual function, `objectID`. When a member function is nonvirtual, it's not supposed to behave differently in derived classes. In fact, a nonvirtual member function specifies an *invariant over specialization*, because it identifies behavior that is not supposed to change, no matter how specialized a derived class becomes. As such,

- The purpose of declaring a nonvirtual function is to have derived classes inherit a function *interface as well as a mandatory implementation.*

You can think of the declaration for `Shape::objectID` as saying, "Every `Shape` object has a function that yields an object identifier, and that object identifier is always computed in the same way. That way is determined by the definition of `Shape::objectID`, and no derived class should try to change how it's done." Because a nonvirtual function identifies an invariant over specialization, it should never be redefined in a subclass, a point that is discussed in detail in Item 37.

The differences in declarations for pure virtual, simple virtual, and nonvirtual functions allow you to specify with fair precision what you want derived classes to inherit: interface only, interface and a default implementation, or interface and a mandatory implementation, respectively. Because these different types of declarations mean fundamentally different things, you must choose carefully among them when you declare your member functions. If you do, you should avoid the two most common mistakes made by inexperienced class designers.

The first mistake is to declare all functions nonvirtual. That leaves no room for specialization in derived classes; nonvirtual destructors are particularly problematic (see Item 14). Of course, it's perfectly reasonable to design a class that is not intended to be used as a base class, and in that case a set of exclusively nonvirtual member functions is appropriate. Too often, however, such classes are declared either out of ignorance of the differences between virtual and nonvirtual functions or as a result of an unsubstantiated concern over the performance cost of virtual functions. The fact of the matter is that almost any class that's to be used as a base class will have virtual functions (again, see Item 14).

If you're concerned about the cost of virtual functions, allow me to bring up the rule of 80-20 (see also Item 33), which states that in a typical program, 80 percent of the runtime will be spent executing just 20 percent of the code. This rule is important, because it means that, on average, 80 percent of your function calls can be virtual without having the slightest detectable impact on your program's performance. Before you go gray worrying about whether you can afford the cost of a virtual function, then, take the simple precaution of making sure that you're focusing on the 20 percent of your program where the decision might really make a difference.

The other common problem is to declare *all* member functions virtual. Sometimes this is actually the right thing to do — witness ABCs, for example — but it can also be the sign of a class designer who lacks the backbone to take a firm stand. Some functions should *not* be redefinable in derived classes, and whenever that's the case, you've got to say so by making those functions nonvirtual. It serves no one to pretend that your class can be all things to all people if they'll just take the time to redefine all your functions. Remember that if you have a base class B, a derived class D, and a member function mf, then each of the following calls to mf *must* work properly:

```
D *pd = new D;
B *pb = pd;

pb->mf();                          // call mf through a
                                   // pointer-to-base

pd->mf();                          // call mf through a
                                   // pointer-to-derived
```

Sometimes, you must make mf a nonvirtual function to ensure that everything behaves the way it's supposed to (see Item 37). If you have an invariant over specialization, don't be afraid to say so!

37 Never redefine an inherited nonvirtual function.

There are two ways of looking at this issue, the theoretical way, and the pragmatic way. Let's start with the pragmatic way. After all, theoreticians are used to being patient.

Suppose I tell you that a class B is publicly derived from a class A, and that there is a public member function mf defined in class A. The parameters and return type of mf are unimportant, so let's just assume they're both void. In other words, I say this:

```
class A {
public:
  void mf();

  ...

};
```

```
class B: public A { ... };
```

Even without knowing anything about A, B, or mf, given an object x of type B,

```
B x;                          // x is an object of type B
```

you would probably be quite surprised if this,

```
A *pA = &x;                   // get pointer to x

pA->mf();                     // call mf through pointer
```

behaved differently than this:

```
B *pB = &x;                   // get pointer to x

pB->mf();                     // call mf through pointer
```

That's because in both cases you're invoking the member function mf on the object x. Because it's the same function and the same object in both cases, it should behave the same way, right?

Right, it should. However, it might not. In particular, it won't if mf is nonvirtual and B has defined its own version of mf:

```
class B: public A {
public:
  void mf();                  // hides A::mf; see Item 50

  ...

};

pA->mf();                     // calls A::mf

pB->mf();                     // calls B::mf
```

The reason for this two-faced behavior is that *nonvirtual* functions like A::mf and B::mf are statically bound (see Item 38). That means that because pA is declared to be of type pointer-to-A, nonvirtual functions invoked through pA will always be those defined for class A, even if pA points to an object of a class derived from A, as it does in this example.

Virtual functions, on the other hand, are dynamically bound (again, see Item 38), and hence don't suffer from this problem. If mf were a virtual function, a call to mf through either pA or pB would result in an invocation of B::mf, because what pA and pB *really* point to is an object of type B.

The bottom line, then, is that if you are writing class B and you redefine a nonvirtual function mf that you inherit from class A, B objects will likely exhibit schizophrenic behavior. In particular, any given B object may act like either an A or a B when mf is called, and the determining factor will have nothing to do with the object itself, but with the declared type of the pointer that points to it. References exhibit the same baffling behavior as do pointers.

So much for the pragmatic argument. What you want now, I know, is some kind of theoretical justification for not redefining inherited non-virtual functions. I am pleased to oblige.

Item 35 explains that public inheritance means isa, and Item 36 describes why declaring a nonvirtual function in a class establishes an invariant over specialization for that class. If you apply these observations to the classes A and B and to the nonvirtual member function A::mf, then

- Everything that is true of A objects is also true of B objects, because every B object isa A object;

- Subclasses of A must inherit both the interface *and* the implementation of mf, because mf is nonvirtual in A.

Now, if B redefines mf, there is a contradiction in your design. If B *really* needs to implement mf differently than A, and if every A object — no matter how specialized — *really* has to use the A implementation for mf, then it's simply not true that every B isa A. In that case, B shouldn't publicly inherit from A. On the other hand, if B *really* has to publicly inherit from A, and if B *really* needs to implement mf differently than A, then it's just not true that mf reflects an invariant over specialization for A. In that case, mf should be virtual. Finally, if every B *really* isa A, and if mf really corresponds to an invariant over specialization for A, then B can't honestly need to redefine mf, and it shouldn't try to do so.

Regardless of which argument applies, something has to give, and under no conditions is it the prohibition on redefining an inherited nonvirtual function.

38 Never redefine an inherited default parameter value.

Let's simplify this discussion right from the start. A default parameter can exist only as part of a function, and you can inherit only two kinds of functions: virtual functions and nonvirtual functions. Therefore, the only way to redefine a default parameter value is to redefine an inherited function. However, it's always a mistake to redefine an inherited nonvirtual function (see Item 37), so we can safely limit our discussion here to the situation in which you inherit a *virtual* function with a default parameter value.

That being the case, the justification for this item becomes quite straightforward: virtual functions are dynamically bound, but default parameter values are statically bound.

What's that? You say you're not up on the latest object-oriented lingo, or perhaps the difference between static and dynamic binding has slipped your already overburdened mind? Let's review, then.

An object's *static type* is the type you declare it to have in the program text. Consider this class hierarchy:

```
enum ShapeColor { RED, GREEN, BLUE };

// a class for geometric shapes
class Shape {
public:
  // all shapes must offer a function to draw them
  virtual void draw(ShapeColor color = RED) const = 0;

  ...

};

class Rectangle: public Shape {
public:
  // notice the different default parameter value - bad!
  virtual void draw(ShapeColor color = GREEN) const;


  ...

};

class Circle: public Shape {
public:
  virtual void draw(ShapeColor color) const;

  ...

};
```

Graphically, it looks like this:

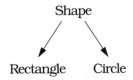

Shape

Rectangle   Circle

Now consider these pointers:

```
Shape *ps1;                        // static type = Shape*

Shape *ps2 = new Circle;           // static type = Shape*

Shape *ps3 = new Rectangle;        // static type = Shape*
```

In this example, ps1, ps2, and ps3 are all declared to be of type pointer-to-Shape, so they all have that as their static type. Notice that

it makes absolutely no difference what they're *really* pointing to —
their static type is Shape* regardless.

An object's *dynamic type* is determined by the type of the object it currently refers to. That is, its dynamic type indicates how it will behave.
In the example above, ps2's dynamic type is Circle*, and ps3's dynamic type is Rectangle*. As for ps1, it doesn't really have a dynamic
type, because it doesn't refer to any object (yet).

Dynamic types, as their name suggests, can change as a program
runs, typically through assignments:

```
ps1 = ps2;                    // ps1's dynamic type is
                              // now Circle*

ps1 = ps3;                    // ps1's dynamic type is
                              // now Rectangle*
```

Virtual functions are *dynamically bound*, meaning that the particular
function called is determined by the dynamic type of the object
through which it's invoked:

```
ps2->draw(RED);               // calls Circle::draw(RED)

ps3->draw(RED);               // calls
                              // Rectangle::draw(RED)
```

This is all old hat, I know: you surely understand virtual functions.
The twist comes in when you consider virtual functions with default
parameter values, because, as I said above, virtual functions are dynamically bound, but default parameters are statically bound. That
means that you may end up invoking a virtual function defined in a *derived class* but using a default parameter value from a *base class*:

```
ps3->draw();                  // calls
                              // Rectangle::draw(RED)!
```

In this case, ps3's dynamic type is Rectangle, so the Rectangle virtual function is called, just as you would expect. In Rectangle::draw,
the default parameter value is GREEN. Because ps3's static type is
Shape, however, the default parameter value for this function call is
taken from the Shape class, not the Rectangle class! The result is a
call consisting of a strange and almost certainly unanticipated combination of the declarations for draw in both the Shape and Rectangle
classes. Trust me when I tell you that you don't want your software to
behave this way, or at least believe me when I tell you that your *clients*
won't want your software to behave this way.

Needless to say, the fact that ps1, ps2, and ps3 are pointers is of no
consequence in this matter. Were they references, the problem would

persist. The only important things are that draw is a virtual function, and one of its default parameter values is redefined in a subclass.

Why does C++ insist on acting in this perverse manner? The answer has to do with runtime efficiency. If default parameter values were dynamically bound, compilers would have to come up with a way of determining the appropriate default value(s) for parameters of virtual functions at runtime, which would be slower and more complicated than the current mechanism of determining them during compilation. The decision was made to err on the side of speed and simplicity of implementation, and the result is that you now enjoy execution behavior that is efficient, but confusing.

39 Avoid casts down the inheritance hierarchy.

In these tumultuous economic times, it's a good idea to keep an eye on our financial institutions, so consider an ABC (see Item 34) for bank accounts:

```
class Person { ... };

class BankAccount {
public:
  BankAccount(const Person *primaryOwner,
              const Person *jointOwner);
  virtual ~BankAccount();

  virtual void makeDeposit(long amount) = 0;
  virtual void makeWithdrawal(long amount) = 0;

  virtual long balance() const = 0;

  ...

};
```

My experience has been that banks rarely distinguish themselves by their broad array of helpful services, so let's assume that there is only one type of bank account, namely, a savings account:

```
class SavingsAccount: public BankAccount {
public:
  SavingsAccount(const Person *primaryOwner,
                 const Person *jointOwner);
  ~SavingsAccount();

  void creditInterest();          // add interest to account

  ...

};
```

This isn't much of a savings account, but then again, what *is* these days? At any rate, it's enough for our purposes.

A bank is likely to keep a list of its accounts, which might be implemented using a list class. Lists are such common data structures that this kind of class is a prime candidate for a template (see Item 49):

```
template<class T>
class List {
public:
  insert(T *pT, int position);
  T * remove(int position);

  T * operator[](int position);
  const T * operator[](int position) const;

  int length() const;

private:

  ...

};
```

If you're confounded by the two different declarations of List::operator[], I respectfully suggest that you consult Item 21.

Suppose the bank has a list of all its accounts, imaginatively named allAccounts,

```
List<BankAccount> allAccounts; // all accounts in the bank
```

and further suppose that you're supposed to write the code to iterate over all the accounts, crediting the interest due to each one. You might try this,

```
// a loop that won't compile
for (int i = 0; i < allAccounts.length(); i++)
  allAccounts[i]->creditInterest();
```

but the compiler would quickly bring you to your senses: the call to allAccounts.operator[] returns a pointer to a BankAccount object, not a SavingsAccount object, so the call to creditInterest is invalid.

This is frustrating. Sure, List<BankAccount>::operator[] is declared to return a BankAccount*, but you *know* that it will actually return a SavingsAccount* in the loop above, because SavingsAccount is the only class that can be instantiated. Stupid compiler! You decide to tell your compiler what you know to be obvious and what the compiler is too dense to figure out on its own: the call to allAccounts.-operator[] really returns a SavingsAccount*:

```
// a loop that will compile, but that is nonetheless evil
for (int i = 0; i < allAccounts.length(); i++)
  ((SavingsAccount*) allAccounts[i])->creditInterest();
```

All your problems are solved! Solved clearly, solved elegantly, solved concisely, all by the simple use of a cast. You know what type of pointer `operator[]` is returning, the compiler doesn't, so you use a cast to tell it. What could be more logical?

There is a biblical analogy I'd like to draw here. Casts are to C++ programmers what the apple was to Eve.

This kind of cast, from a base class pointer to a subclass pointer, is called a *downcast*, because you're casting down the inheritance hierarchy. In the example you just looked at, downcasting happens to work, but it leads to a maintenance nightmare, as you will soon see. Before examining the maintenance implications, however, it's worth noting that downcasting from a *virtual* base class is *always* illegal, so changing `SavingsAccount` to be declared as follows would have the side-effect of breaking the loop containing the cast:

```
class SavingsAccount: virtual public BankAccount { ... };
```

As a result, you don't want to get too comfortable with the idea of downcasting your way out of trouble (an oxymoron anyway), because the trick fails completely in the presence of virtual base classes (see Item 43).

But back to the bank and the maintenance repercussions of downcasting. Buoyed by the success of its savings accounts, let's suppose the bank, in an unprecedented demonstration of competitive initiative, decides to introduce checking accounts. Furthermore, assume that checking accounts also bear interest, just like savings accounts:

```
class CheckingAccount: public BankAccount {
public:
  void creditInterest();         // add interest to account

  ...

};
```

Needless to say, `allAccounts` will now be a list containing both savings and checking accounts. Suddenly, the interest-crediting loop you wrote above is in serious trouble.

Your first problem is that it will continue to compile even without your changing it to reflect the existence of `CheckingAccount` objects, because the compiler will *believe* you when you tell it that all-Accounts.operator[] really returns a `SavingsAccount*`. After all, you're the boss. That's Maintenance Nightmare Number One. Maintenance Nightmare Number Two is what you're tempted to do to fix the problem, which is typically to write code like this:

```
for (int i = 0; i < allAccounts.length(); i++) {
  if (allAccounts[i] is of type SavingsAccount*)
    ((SavingsAccount*) allAccounts[i])->creditInterest();
  else
    ((CheckingAccount*) allAccounts[i])->creditInterest();
}
```

Fortunately, C++ provides no way to determine at runtime the actual type of object a pointer points to, and let me assure you that that's no accident. In fact, runtime type inquiry was explicitly omitted from the language to prevent abuses just such as this.

Anytime you find yourself writing code of the form, "if the object is of type T1, then do something, but if it's of type T2, then do something else," slap yourself. That isn't The C++ Way. Yes, it's a reasonable strategy in C, in Pascal, even in Smalltalk, but not in C++. In C++, you use virtual functions.

Remember that with a virtual function, the *compiler* is responsible for making sure that the right function is called, depending on the type of the object being used. Don't litter your code with conditionals or switch statements; let the compiler do the work for you. Here's how:

```
class BankAccount { ... };      // as above

// new class representing accounts that bear interest
class InterestBearingAccount: public BankAccount {
public:
  virtual void creditInterest() = 0;

  ...

};

class SavingsAccount: public InterestBearingAccount {

  ...                             // as above

};

class CheckingAccount: public InterestBearingAccount {

  ...                             // as above

};
```

Graphically, it looks like this:

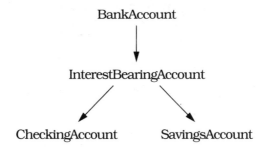

Because both savings and checking accounts earn interest, you'd naturally like to move that common behavior up into a common base class. However, under the assumption that not all accounts in the bank will necessarily bear interest (certainly a valid assumption in my experience), you can't move it into the BankAccount class. As a result, you've introduced a new subclass of BankAccount called Interest-BearingAccount, and you've made SavingsAccount and Checking-Account inherit from it.

The fact that both savings and checking accounts bear interest is indicated by the InterestBearingAccount pure virtual function creditInterest, which is presumably redefined in its subclasses SavingsAccount and CheckingAccount.

This new class hierarchy allows you to rewrite your loop as follows:

```
// better, but still not perfect
for (int i = 0; i < allAccounts.length(); i++)
  ((InterestBearingAccount*) allAccounts[i])->creditInterest();
```

Although this loop still contains a nasty little cast, it's much more robust than it used to be, because it will continue to work even if new subclasses of InterestBearingAccount are added to your application.

To get rid of the cast entirely, you must make some additional changes to your design. One approach is to tighten up the specification of your list of accounts. If you could get a list of InterestBearingAccount objects instead of BankAccount objects, then everything would be peachy:

```
// all interest-bearing accounts in the bank
List<InterestBearingAccount> allIBAccounts;

// a loop that compiles and works, both now and forever
for (int i = 0; i < allIBAccounts.length(); i++)
  allIBAccounts[i]->creditInterest();
```

If getting a more specialized list isn't an option, it might make sense to say that the creditInterest operation applies to *all* bank accounts, but that for non-interest-bearing accounts, it's just a no-op. That could be expressed this way:

```
class BankAccount {
public:
  virtual void creditInterest() {}

  ...

};

class SavingsAccount: public BankAccount { ... };

class CheckingAccount: public BankAccount { ... };

List<BankAccount> allAccounts;

// look ma, no cast!
for (int i = 0; i < allAccounts.length(); i++)
  allAccounts[i]->creditInterest();
```

Notice that the virtual function BankAccount::creditInterest provides an empty default implementation. This is a convenient way to specify that its behavior is a no-op by default, but that can lead to unforeseen difficulties in its own right. For the inside story on why, as well as how to eliminate the danger, consult Item 36.

As you have seen, downcasts can be eliminated in a number of ways. The best way is to replace such casts with calls to virtual functions, possibly also making each virtual function a no-op for any classes to which it doesn't truly apply. A second method is to tighten up the typing so that there is no ambiguity between the declared type of a pointer and the pointer type that you know is really there.

Whatever the effort required to get rid of downcasts, it's effort well spent, because downcasts are error-prone, fragile, and, in the case of virtual base classes, flat-out illegal.

What I've just written is the truth and nothing but the truth; it is not, however, the whole truth. It's somewhat embarrassing to admit it, but there are in fact rare occasions when you really *do* have to perform a downcast. Nonetheless, there is a better way to do it than through a raw C++ cast such as you saw above. The better way is called "safe downcasting," and you implement it in terms of — surprise! — virtual functions.

Safe downcasting applies only to pointers, and the scheme is amazingly simple. If you have a pointer to a base class, and you'd like to turn it into a pointer to a derived class, you call a virtual function to actually do the cast. The return value of the function is either zero, in which case the cast failed, or nonzero, in which case the returned value is a valid pointer to the derived class.

Here's the banking example with safe downcasting added:

```
class SavingsAccount;          // forward declaration
class CheckingAccount;         // forward declaration

class BankAccount {
public:
  virtual void creditInterest() {}

  virtual SavingsAccount * castToSavingsAccount()
  { return 0; }

  virtual CheckingAccount * castToCheckingAccount()
  { return 0; }

  ...

};

class SavingsAccount: public BankAccount {
public:
  SavingsAccount * castToSavingsAccount()
  { return this; }

  ...

};

class CheckingAccount: public BankAccount {
public:
  CheckingAccount * castToCheckingAccount()
  { return this; }

  ...

};
```

The base class BankAccount declares two new functions for safe downcasting, castToSavingsAccount and castToCheckingAccount; notice that each returns the appropriate pointer type. Also notice how the classes SavingsAccount and CheckingAccount must be mentioned prior to the BankAccount class declaration — this is so the compiler knows that SavingsAccount and CheckingAccount are class names when it encounters the declarations for the safe downcasting functions. Finally, notice that the default implementation for the safe downcasts is to return 0, the null pointer. By default, the downcasts will fail.

Each derived class redefines only the safe downcast for its class, and the implementation is trivial: just return this. Within a member function of a class, you know that this points to an object of that class, so the implementation is safe.

You use safe downcasts like this:

```
void error(const char *msg);    // error-handling function

List<BankAccount> allAccounts;

// well, ma, at least the casts are safe...
for (int i = 0; i < allAccounts.length(); i++) {
  SavingsAccount *psa;
  CheckingAccount *pca;

  // try safe-downcasting allAccounts[i] to a SavingsAccount
  if (psa = allAccounts[i]->castToSavingsAccount())
    psa->creditInterest();

  // try safe-downcasting it to a CheckingAccount
  else if (pca = allAccounts[i]->castToCheckingAccount())
    pca->creditInterest();

  // uh oh -- unknown account type
  else
    error("Unknown account type!");
}
```

This scheme is far from ideal, but at least you can detect it when your downcasts fail, something that's impossible with built-in C++ casts. Also, safe downcasting can be implemented for *any* base class, including virtual bases, something else that raw C++ casts can't match. Nevertheless, the if-then-else style of programming that downcasting invariably leads to is vastly inferior to the use of virtual functions, and you should reserve it for situations in which you truly have no alternative. With any luck, you will never face such a bleak and desolate programming landscape.

40 Model "has-a" or "is-implemented-in-terms-of" through layering.

Layering is the process of building one class on top of another class by having the layering class contain an object of the layered class as a data member. For example:

```
class String { ... };          // character strings

class Address { ... };         // where someone lives

class PhoneNumber { ... };

class Person {
private:
  String name;                 // layered object
  Address address;             // ditto
  PhoneNumber voiceNumber;     // ditto
  PhoneNumber faxNumber;       // ditto
```

```
public:

    ...

};
```

In this example, the `Person` class is said to be layered on top of the `String`, `Address`, and `PhoneNumber` classes, because it contains data members of those types. Layering is also known as *containment* or *embedding*.

Item 35 explains that public inheritance means "isa." In contrast, layering means either "has-a" or "is-implemented-in-terms-of."

The `Person` class above demonstrates the has-a relationship. A `Person` object has a name, an address, and telephone numbers for both voice and FAX communication. You wouldn't say that a person *is* a string or that a person *is* an address, you would say that a person *has* a string and *has* an address, etc. Most people have little difficulty with this distinction, and confusion between the roles of isa and has-a is relatively rare.

Somewhat more troublesome is the difference between isa and is-implemented-in-terms-of. For example, suppose that you have a class that implements linked lists of objects. Such a class is an ideal candidate for a template (see Item 49):

```
template<class T>
class LinkedList {
private:

    ...                             // implementation is
                                    // unimportant
public:
  LinkedList();
  LinkedList(const LinkedList& rhs);
  virtual ~LinkedList();

  LinkedList& operator=(const LinkedList& rhs);

  virtual void insert(T& item, int position);
  virtual T& remove(int position);

  virtual T& operator[](int position);
  virtual const T& operator[](int position) const;

  int length() const;
};
```

This class offers basic list operations, including construction, destruction (see Item 14), assignment (see Item 15), pass-by-value (via the copy constructor), insertion and removal of items, access to items by position (see Item 21 for a discussion of why there are two versions), and determination of the number of elements in the list.

Now suppose that your real goal is to develop a template class to represent sets of items of type T, where a set is, as usual, an unordered collection without duplicates. Being the data structure maven that you are, you know that of the nearly limitless choices for implementing sets, one particularly simple way is to employ linked lists. Because you have a linked list class already written, you decide to engage in a little code reuse by having your nascent Set class inherit from LinkedList. After all, in your implementation, a Set object will in fact *be* a LinkedList object. Your decision is further buttressed by the fact that the LinkedList class is clearly designed to be a base class: notice the virtual functions, including, significantly, the virtual destructor (see Item 14).

Hence, you declare your Set class like this:

```
// the wrong way to associate sets and linked lists
template<class T>
class Set: public LinkedList<T> { ... };
```

Everything may seem fine and dandy at this point, but in fact there is something quite wrong. As Item 35 explains, if B isa A, then everything that is true of A is also true of B. However, a LinkedList object is an *ordered* collection, a fact made plain by the presence of the operator[] functions that take a position argument in the LinkedList class. In contrast, a Set is an *unordered* collection, and the operator[] functions it inherits from LinkedList make no sense for it. It is *not* true that a Set isa LinkedList, because some of the things that are true for LinkedList objects are not true for Set objects.

Because the relationship between these two classes isn't isa, public inheritance is the wrong way to model that relationship. The right way to model that relationship is to realize that a Set object can be *implemented in terms of* a LinkedList object:

```
// the right way to associate sets and linked lists
template<class T>
class Set {
private:
  LinkedList<T> rep;              // representation for a set

public:
  int member(const T& item) const;

  void insert(T& item);
  void remove(const T& item);

  int cardinality() const;
};
```

If you implement Set::member such that it returns 0 if the given item is not in the set and nonzero otherwise (following the usual C++ convention), and if you, as class implementer, know that any nonzero value returned is actually one greater than the position of the given item in the underlying LinkedList object (i.e., if member returns *n*, the position of item in the underlying linked list is *n-1*), then you can write the other Set member functions as trivial inline functions (see Item 33):

```
template<class T>
inline void Set<T>::insert(T& item)
{
  if (!member(item))            // assume position 0 of rep
    rep.insert(item, 0);        // is front of the list
}

template<class T>
inline void Set<T>::remove(const T& item)
{
  int position = member(item);
  if (position) rep.remove(position-1);
}

template<class T>
inline int Set<T>::cardinality() const
{ return rep.length(); }
```

Notice how the use of layering keeps inappropriate functions defined in the LinkedList class such as operator[] out of the interface of the Set class; this would not be possible had you tried to use public inheritance. Also notice how you still achieve code reuse. You gain the benefits of all the code in the LinkedList class, but instead of inheriting it, you call it explicitly through your (very simple) member functions.

As an aside, the Set class interface fails the test of being complete and minimal (see Item 18). In terms of completeness, the primary omission is that of a way to iterate over the contents of a set, something that might well be necessary for many applications. Furthermore, the functions union, intersection, difference, etc., are conventionally defined for sets, and these too are missing. Given an iteration capability, the functions union, intersection, difference, etc., would no longer be part of a minimal interface, but they are of sufficient importance that it would nonetheless be prudent to provide them.

41 Use private inheritance judiciously.

Item 35 demonstrates that C++ treats public inheritance as an isa relationship by showing that, given a hierarchy in which a class Student publicly inherits from a class Person, the compiler implicitly converts

`Student` pointers to `Person` pointers when it is necessary for a call to succeed. It's worth repeating a portion of that example using private inheritance instead of public inheritance:

```
class Person { ... };

class Student:                  // this time we use
  private Person { ... };       // private inheritance

void dance(const Person& p);    // anyone can dance

void study(const Student& s);   // only students study

Person p;                       // p is a Person
Student s;                      // s is a Student

dance(p);                       // fine, p is a Person

dance(s);                       // error! a Student isn't
                                // a Person
```

Clearly, private inheritance doesn't mean isa. What does it mean then?

"Whoa!," you say. "Before we get to the meaning, let's cover the behavior. How does private inheritance behave?" Well, the first rule governing private inheritance you've just seen in action: in contrast to public inheritance, the compiler will *not* convert a pointer to a derived class object (such as `Student`) into a pointer to a base class object (such as `Person`) if the inheritance relationship between the classes is private. That's why the call to `dance` fails for the object `s`. The second rule is that members inherited from a private base class become private members of the derived class, even if they were protected or public in the base class. So much for behavior.

That brings us to meaning, and private inheritance means is-implemented-in-terms-of. If you make a class B privately inherit from a class A, you do so because you are interested in taking advantage of some of the code that has already been written for class A, not because there is any deep conceptual relationship between objects of type A and objects of type B. As such, private inheritance is purely an implementation technique. Using the terms introduced in Item 36, private inheritance means that implementation *only* should be inherited; interface should be ignored. If B privately inherits from A, it means that B objects are implemented in terms of A objects, nothing more. Private inheritance means nothing during software *design*, only during software *implementation*.

The fact that private inheritance means is-implemented-in-terms-of is a little disturbing, because Item 40 points out that layering can mean the same thing. How are you supposed to choose between them? The answer is simple: use layering whenever you can, use private inheritance if you have to. When do you have to? When protected members and/or virtual functions enter the picture — but more on that in a moment.

Item 40 shows how to implement a class Set in terms of a class LinkedList by layering a LinkedList object inside each Set object. You should familiarize yourself with that example now, and then contrast the layering approach with the one below, which uses private inheritance:

```
template<class T>
class Set: private LinkedList<T> {
public:
  int member(const T& item) const;

  void insert(T& item);
  void remove(const T& item);

  int cardinality() const;
};

template<class T>
inline void Set<T>::insert(T& item)
{
  // assume position 0 is front of the linked list
  if (!member(item))
    LinkedList<T>::insert(item, 0);
}

template<class T>
inline void Set<T>::remove(const T& item)
{
  int position = member(item);
  if (position) LinkedList<T>::remove(position-1);
}

template<class T>
inline int Set<T>::cardinality() const
{ return length(); }
```

As you can see, the implementations of the Set member functions using private inheritance are nearly identical to those using layering. The primary difference is that this example calls the LinkedList functions insert, remove, and length directly (because they are inherited) instead of going through an embedded object. Also, Set::insert must explicitly call the LinkedList version of insert; otherwise Set::insert would be infinitely recursive, an implementation strategy of little utility and not much more entertainment value. A similar argument applies to Set::remove.

However, suppose that Set were part of a *public* inheritance hierarchy, too. For example, the Set class might publicly inherit from a general

UnorderedCollection template class. If that were the case — and it hardly seems necessary to point out that in an object-oriented program, many classes will be part of an isa hierarchy — then Set would have to be declared like this:

```
template<class T>
class Set: public UnorderedCollection<T>,
           private LinkedList<T> { ... };
```

Uh oh, multiple inheritance. Multiple inheritance is examined in laborious detail in Item 43, but for our purposes here, suffice it to say that you don't want to get involved with it if you don't have to.

In this case, of course, you don't have to, because you can use layering instead of private inheritance. This is frequently possible, and whenever you can take advantage of it, you should. Layering is always to be preferred over private inheritance, because it simplifies your life. Well, maybe it doesn't exactly simplify your *life*, but it certainly simplifies your code.

Sometimes, however, the simplification isn't possible. In particular, if your class needs access to protected members of a base class, or if it needs to redefine virtual functions, you haven't got a choice, you *must* use inheritance.

For example, Item 11 describes why writing correct copy constructors and assignment operators for classes with dynamically allocated memory can be tricky, and it should be apparent that the LinkedList class is pretty darn likely to be doing some dynamic memory allocation. That being the case, and in recognition of the subtle issues involved, the designer of the LinkedList class might decide to protect the copy constructor and the assignment operator, disallowing their use by general clients, but making them accessible to writers of derived classes:

```
template<class T>
class LinkedList {
protected:
  LinkedList(const LinkedList& rhs);
  LinkedList& operator=(const LinkedList& rhs);

  ...                            // otherwise as in Item 40

};
```

For your Set class, suppose that you want to allow clients to copy and assign to Set objects at will, and further suppose that you want to rely on the implementations in the LinkedList class for those operations. To do that, you need access to the protected members of LinkedList, so you have no choice of implementation strategy: you *must* use private inheritance:

```
template<class T>
class Set: private LinkedList<T> {
public:
  Set& operator=(const Set& rhs);

  ...

};
template<class T>
Set<T>& Set<T>::operator=(const Set<T>& rhs)
{
  if (this == &rhs)                // see Item 17
    return *this;                  // see Item 15

  LinkedList<T>::operator=(rhs);
                                   // see Item 16

  return *this;                    // see Item 15
}
```

Notice how the Set class, in order to allow copying, does ... *nothing*. "How," you may wonder, "do Set class clients get access to the protected LinkedList copy constructor?"

The answer is that they get access to it via the Set copy constructor. "But there is no Set copy constructor!," you protest. Ah, but there is. Recall that the compiler generates one for you if you don't write a copy constructor of your own. (If this is news to you, see Item 45.) That (compiler-generated) copy constructor causes calls to be made to the LinkedList copy constructor, but those calls are valid, because they're charged to the Set copy constructor, which has access to the protected members of the LinkedList class because it's a member function of a derived class. Pretty straightforward, in a Byzantine sort of way, huh?

Now, you can sit back and let the compiler play the same game with the assignment operator, because that function will be implicitly generated, too (see Item 45), but perhaps you want to detect assignments to self as early as possible (see Item 17). If so, you must write your own assignment operator as shown above.

The most important insight to carry away from this example is that it could not have been implemented using layering. Only inheritance gives access to protected members, and only inheritance allows for virtual functions to be redefined. Because virtual functions and protected members exist, private inheritance is sometimes the only practical way to express an is-implemented-in-terms-of relationship between classes. As a result, you shouldn't be afraid to use private inheritance when it's the most appropriate implementation technique at your disposal. At the same time, however, layering is the preferable technique in general, so you should employ it whenever you can.

42 Differentiate between inheritance and templates.

Consider the following two design problems:

- Being a devoted student of computer science, you want to design a class representing stacks of objects. You'll actually need a collection of different classes, because each stack must be homogeneous, i.e., it must have only a single type of object in it. For example, you might have a class for stacks of ints, a second class for stacks of strings, a third for stacks of complex numbers, perhaps a fourth for stacks of stacks of strings, etc. You're only interested in supporting a minimal interface to the class (see Item 18), so the only operations you'll support are creation, destruction, pushing a new object on top of the stack, and popping the top object off the stack.

- Being a devoted feline aficionado, you want to design a class representing cats. You'll actually need a collection of different classes, because each species of cat is a little different. Like all objects, cats can be created and destroyed, but, as any cat-lover knows, the only other things cats do are eat and sleep. However, each species of cat eats and sleeps in its own endearing way.

These two problem specifications sound remarkably similar, yet they result in utterly different software designs. Why?

The answer has to do with the relationship between each class's behavior and the *type* of object being manipulated. With both stacks and cats, you're dealing with a variety of different types (stacks containing objects of type T, cats of species T), but the question you must ask yourself is this: does the type T actually affect the *behavior* of the class? If T does *not* affect the behavior, you can use a template. If T *does* affect the behavior, you'll need virtual functions, and you'll therefore use inheritance.

Here's how you might declare a linked-list implementation of the Stack class, assuming that the objects to be stacked are of type T:

```
class Stack {
private:
  struct StackNode {          // linked list node
    T data;                   // data at this node
    StackNode *next;          // next node in list
```

```
    // StackNode constructor initializes both fields
    StackNode(const T& newData, StackNode *nextNode)
    : data(newData), next(nextNode) {}
  };

  StackNode *top;                    // top of stack
public:
  Stack();
  ~Stack();

  void push(const T& object);
  T pop();
};
```

The linked list itself is made up of StackNode objects, but that's an implementation detail of the Stack class, so StackNode has been declared a private type of Stack. If your compiler doesn't support nested types yet (see Item 49), don't worry about it — StackNode might just as well have been global. If it were global, however, you'd need to come up with another way of limiting access to it. Probably the easiest way to do that would be to make it a class instead of a struct, to make all of its members private (to prevent general access to them), and to declare Stack a friend (so it would have access), like this:

```
class StackNode {             // global approximation of
private:                      // a private nested class
  T data;
  StackNode *next;

  StackNode(const T& newData, StackNode *nextNode)
  : data(newData), next(nextNode) {}

friend class Stack;
};
```

Notice, by the way, that StackNode has a constructor to make sure all its fields are initialized properly. Just because you can write linked lists in your sleep is no reason to omit technological advances such as constructors. Also, notice that StackNode's constructor is private. If you've ever wondered if it ever made sense for a constructor to be private, now you can stop wondering.

Here is how you might implement the Stack member functions:

```
Stack::Stack(): top(0) {}        // initialize top to nil
```

```
void Stack::push(const T& object)
{
  // put new node at front of list
  top = new StackNode(object, top);

  // check for memory allocation failure (see Item 7)
  if (!top) throw "No More Memory";
}

T Stack::pop()
{
  // check for empty stack
  if (!top) throw "Attempt to pop empty stack";

  StackNode *topOfStack = top;  // remember top node
  top = top->next;

  T data = topOfStack->data;    // remember node data
  delete topOfStack;

  return data;
}

Stack::~Stack()                  // delete all in stack
{
  while (top) {
    StackNode *toDie = top;      // get ptr to top node
    top = top->next;             // move to next node
    delete toDie;                // delete former top node
  }
}
```

These implementations are pretty straightforward, except for the throw expressions inside push and pop, which are used for signaling exceptions (see Item 49). Most compilers don't support exceptions yet, so Item 49 describes a number of ways to limp along until your compiler does support exceptions.

Nested classes and exceptions aside, the main reason that this implementation is interesting is this: you are able to write each member function without knowing *anything* about T. The code you write for construction, for pushing, for popping, and for destruction is the same, no matter what T is; the behavior of a stack does not depend on T at all. That's the hallmark of a template class: the behavior doesn't depend on the type at all.

Turning your Stack class declaration into a real template, by the way, is so simple, even a manager could do it:

```
template<class T> class Stack {

    ...                          // exactly the same as above

};
```

For details on templates, see Item 49. For a sketch of how to simulate them using the preprocessor (a reasonable kludge until your compiler supports them), see Item 1.

But on to cats. Why won't templates work with cats?

Reread the specification, and note the requirement that "each species of cat eats and sleeps in its own endearing way." That means that you're going to have to implement *different behavior* for each type of cat. You can't just write a single function to handle all cats, all you can do is *specify an interface* for a function that each type of cat must implement. Aha! The way to propagate a function *interface only* is to declare a pure virtual function (see Item 36):

```
class Cat {
public:
  virtual ~Cat();                 // see Item 14

  virtual void eat() = 0;         // all cats must eat
  virtual void sleep() = 0;       // all cats must sleep
};
```

Subclasses of Cat — say, Siamese and BritishShortHairedTabby — must of course redefine the eat and sleep function interfaces that they inherit:

```
class Siamese: public Cat {
public:
  void eat();
  void sleep();

  ...

};

class BritishShortHairedTabby: public Cat {
public:
  void eat();
  void sleep();

  ...

};
```

Okay, you now know why templates work for the Stack class and why they won't work for the Cat class. You also know why inheritance works for the Cat class, so the only remaining question is why inheritance won't work for the Stack class. To see why, try to declare the root class of a Stack hierarchy, the single class from which all other stack classes would inherit:

```
class Stack {                       // a stack of anything
public:
  virtual void push(const ??? object) = 0;
  virtual ??? pop() = 0;

  ...

};
```

Now the difficulty becomes clear: what types are you going to declare for the pure virtual functions push and pop? Remember that each subclass must redeclare the virtual functions it inherits *exactly* as they are declared in the base class. Unfortunately, a stack of ints will want to push and pop int objects, whereas a stack of, say, Cats, will want to push and pop Cat objects. How can the Stack class declare its pure virtual functions in such a way that clients can create both stacks of ints and stacks of Cats? The cold, hard truth is that it can't, and that's why inheritance is unsuitable for creating stacks.

But maybe you're the sneaky type. Maybe you think you can outsmart the compiler by using generic (void*) pointers. As it turns out, generic pointers don't help you here. You simply can't get around the requirement that a virtual function's declaration in derived classes must precisely match its declaration in a base class. However, generic pointers can help with a different problem.

It may have occurred to you that templates are essentially just a special-purpose mechanism for macro expansion. If you instantiate a template a dozen times, you are likely to instantiate the *code* for the template functions a dozen times. If the template functions could in fact share code, you are being penalized for using templates; the price is duplicated code. Perhaps you don't want to pay this price.

For certain kinds of classes, you can use generic pointers to avoid the fee. The classes to which this approach is applicable store *pointers* instead of objects, and they are implemented by:

1. Creating a single class that stores void* pointers to objects.

2. Creating a set of additional classes whose only purpose is to enforce strong typing; these classes all use the generic class of step 1 for the actual work.

Here's an example using the Stack class, except that now it has been modified to store generic pointers instead of objects:

```
class GenericStack {
private:
  struct StackNode {
    void *data;                 // data at this node
    StackNode *next;            // next node in list
```

```
    StackNode(void *newData, StackNode *nextNode)
     : data(newData), next(nextNode) {}
  };

  StackNode *top;              // top of stack
public:
  GenericStack();
  ~GenericStack();

  void push(const void *object);
  void * pop();
};
```

Because this class stores pointers instead of objects, it has to take into account the possibility that a single object is pointed to by *more than one stack*. Contrary to what you might think, then, it is of critical importance that pop and the class destructor *not* delete the data pointer of any StackNode object they destroy, although it is of course important that they delete the StackNode object itself. After all, the Stack-Node objects are allocated inside the GenericStack class, so they must also be deallocated inside that class. Surprisingly, then, the implementation of the Stack class you saw earlier suffices almost perfectly for the GenericStack class. The only changes you need to make involve substitutions of void* for T.

The GenericStack class by itself is of little utility — it's too easy to misuse. For example, a client could mistakenly push a pointer to a Cat object onto a stack meant to hold only pointers to ints, and the compiler would merrily accept it. After all, a pointer's a pointer when it comes to void* parameters.

To regain the type safety to which you have become accustomed, you create *interface classes* to GenericStack, like this:

```
class IntStack {                 // interface class for ints
private:
  GenericStack s;                // implementation

public:
  void push(int *intPtr) { s.push(intPtr); }
  int * pop() { return (int *) s.pop(); }
};
class CatStack {                 // interface class for cats
private:
  GenericStack s;                // implementation

public:
  void push(Cat *catPtr) { s.push(catPtr); }
  Cat * pop() { return (Cat *) s.pop(); }
};
```

As you can see, the `IntStack` and `CatStack` classes serve only to en-force strong typing. Only `int` pointers can be pushed onto an `IntStack` or popped from it, and only `Cat` pointers can be pushed onto a `CatStack` or popped from it. Both `IntStack` and `CatStack` are im-plemented in terms of the class `GenericStack`, a relationship that is expressed through layering (see Item 40), and `IntStack` and `Cat-Stack` will share the code for the functions in `GenericStack` that ac-tually implement their behavior.

As is pointed out in Item 41, the other way to state an is-implemented-in-terms-of relationship between classes is through private inherit-ance. In this case, that technique offers an advantage over layering, because it allows you to express the fact that the `GenericStack` class is too unsafe for general use; it should be used only to implement other classes. You say that by protecting `GenericStack`'s member func-tions:

```
class GenericStack {
private:

    ...                                // same as above

protected:
  GenericStack();
  ~GenericStack();

  void push(const void *object);
  void * pop();
};

class IntStack: private GenericStack {
public:
  void push(int *intPtr) { GenericStack::push(intPtr); }
  int * pop() { return (int *) GenericStack::pop(); }
};

class CatStack: private GenericStack {
public:
  void push(Cat *catPtr) { GenericStack::push(catPtr); }
  Cat * pop() { return (Cat *) GenericStack::pop(); }
};
```

Like the layering approach, of course, the implementation based on private inheritance avoids needless code duplication.

Building type-safe interfaces on top of the `GenericStack` class is a pretty slick maneuver, but it's still awfully unpleasant to have to type in all those interface classes by hand. Fortunately, you don't have to — you can use templates. Here's a template to generate type-safe inter-faces using private inheritance:

```
template<class T>
class Stack: private GenericStack {
public:
  void push(T *objectPtr) { GenericStack::push(objectPtr); }
  T * pop() { return (T *) GenericStack::pop(); }
};
```

All in all, pretty nifty, huh?

Yet let's not lose sight of the forest for the trees, nifty though they may be. The primary lessons to be learned are these:

- Templates should be used to generate a collection of classes when the type of the objects *does not* affect the behavior of the class's functions.

- Inheritance should be used with a collection of classes when the type of the objects *does* affect the behavior of the class's functions.

43 Use multiple inheritance judiciously.

Depending on who's doing the talking, multiple inheritance (MI) is either the product of divine inspiration or the manifest work of the devil. Proponents hail it as essential to the natural modeling of real-world problems, while critics argue that it is slow, difficult to implement, and no more powerful than single inheritance. More disconcerting still, the world of object-oriented programming languages remains split on the issue: C++, Eiffel, and the Common LISP Object System (CLOS) offer MI, while Smalltalk, Objective C, and Object Pascal do not. What's a poor, struggling programmer to believe?

Before you believe anything, you need to get your facts straight. The one indisputable fact about MI in C++ is that it opens up a Pandora's box of complexities that simply do not exist under single inheritance. Of these, the most basic is ambiguity (see Item 26). If a derived class inherits a member name from more than one base class, any reference to that name is inherently ambiguous; you must explicitly say which member you mean. Here's an example from the ARM (see Item 50):

```
class Lottery {
public:
  virtual int draw();

  ...

};
```

```
class GraphicalObject {
public:
  virtual int draw();

  ...

};

class LotterySimulation: public Lottery,
                         public GraphicalObject {

  ...                             // doesn't declare draw

};

LotterySimulation *pls = new LotterySimulation;

pls->draw();                       // error! - ambiguous
pls->Lottery::draw();              // fine
pls->GraphicalObject::draw();      // fine
```

This looks clumsy, but at least it works. Unfortunately, the clumsiness is difficult to eliminate. Even if one of the inherited draw functions were private and hence inaccessible, the ambiguity would remain. (It turns out that there's a good reason for that, but a complete explanation of the situation is provided in Item 26, so I won't repeat it here.)

Explicitly qualifying members is more than clumsy, however, it's also quite limiting. When you explicitly qualify a virtual function with a class name, the function doesn't act virtual any longer. Instead, the function called is precisely the one you specify, even if the object on which it's invoked is of a derived class:

```
class SpecialLotterySimulation: public LotterySimulation {
public:
  virtual int draw();

  ...

};

pls = new SpecialLotterySimulation;

pls->draw();                       // error! - still ambiguous
pls->Lottery::draw();              // calls Lottery::draw
pls->GraphicalObject::draw();      // calls GraphicalObject::draw
```

In this case, notice that even though pls points to a SpecialLotterySimulation object, there is no convenient way (short of a downcast — see Item 39) to invoke the draw function defined in that class.

But wait, there's more. The draw functions in both Lottery and GraphicalObject are declared virtual so that subclasses can redefine them (see Item 36), but what if LotterySimulation would like to redefine *both* of them? The unpleasant truth is that it can't, because a class is allowed to have only a single function called draw that takes no arguments. (There is a special exception to this rule if one of the functions is const and one is not — see Item 21.)

At one point this difficulty was considered a serious enough problem to justify a change in the language — the ARM discusses the possibility of allowing inherited virtual functions to be "renamed" — but then it was discovered that the problem can be circumvented by the addition of a pair of new classes:

```
class AuxLottery: public Lottery {
public:
  virtual int lotteryDraw() = 0;

  virtual int draw() { return lotteryDraw(); }
};

class AuxGraphicalObject: public GraphicalObject {
public:
  virtual int graphicalObjectDraw() = 0;

  virtual int draw() { return graphicalObjectDraw(); }
};

class LotterySimulation: public AuxLottery,
                         public AuxGraphicalObject {
public:
  virtual int lotteryDraw();
  virtual int graphicalObjectDraw();

  ...

};
```

Each of the two new classes, AuxLottery and AuxGraphicalObject, essentially declares a new name for the draw function that each inherits. This new name takes the form of a pure virtual function, in this case lotteryDraw and graphicalObjectDraw; the functions are pure virtual so that concrete subclasses must redefine them. Furthermore, each class redefines the draw that it inherits to itself invoke the new pure virtual function. The net effect is that within this class hierarchy, the single, ambiguous name draw has effectively been split into two unambiguous, but operationally equivalent names, lotteryDraw and graphicalObjectDraw.:

```
LotterySimulation *pls = new LotterySimulation;

Lottery *pl = pls;
GraphicalObject *pgo = pls;

// this calls LotterySimulation::lotteryDraw
pl->draw();
```

```
// this calls LotterySimulation::graphicalObjectDraw
pgo->draw();
```

This strategy, replete as it is with the clever application of pure virtual, simple virtual, and inline functions, should be committed to memory. In the first place, it solves a problem that you may encounter some day. In the second place, it can serve to remind you of the complications that can arise in the presence of multiple inheritance. Yes, this tactic works, but do you really want to be forced to introduce new classes just so you can redefine a virtual function? The classes Aux-Lottery and AuxGraphicalObject are absolutely essential to the correct operation of this hierarchy, but they correspond neither to an abstraction in the problem domain nor to an abstraction in the implementation domain. They exist purely as an implementation device, nothing more. You already know that good software is "device independent"; that rule of thumb applies here, too.

The ambiguity problem, interesting though it is, hardly begins to scratch the surface of the issues you'll confront when you flirt with MI. Another one grows out of the empirical observation that an inheritance hierarchy that starts out looking like this,

```
class B { ... };
class C { ... };
class D: public B, public C { ... };
```

has a distressing tendency to mutate into one that looks like this:

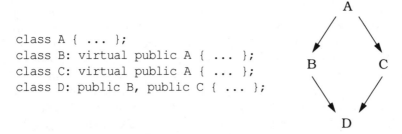

```
class A { ... };
class B: virtual public A { ... };
class C: virtual public A { ... };
class D: public B, public C { ... };
```

Now, it may or may not be true that diamonds are a girl's best friend, but it is certainly true that a diamond-shaped inheritance hierarchy such as this is *not* very friendly. For example, an object of type D may have up to four different addresses, as is explained in Item 17.

If you create a hierarchy such as this, you are immediately confronted with the question of whether to make A a virtual base class. In practice, the answer is invariably that you should; almost never will you want an object of type D to contain multiple copies of the data members of A. In recognition of this truth, B and C above declare A as a virtual base class.

Unfortunately, at the time when you declare B and C, you may not know whether any class will decide to inherit from both of them, and in fact you shouldn't need to know this in order to declare them correctly. As a class designer, this puts you in a dreadful quandary. If you do *not* declare A as a virtual base of B and C, a later designer of D may need to modify the declarations of B and C in order to use them effectively. Frequently, this is unacceptable, often because the declarations of A, B, and C are read-only. This would be the case if A, B, and C were in a library, for example, and D was being written by a library client.

On the other hand, if you *do* declare A as a virtual base of B and C, you almost certainly impose an additional cost in both space and time on clients of those classes. That is because virtual base classes are typically implemented as *pointers* to objects, rather than as objects themselves. It goes without saying that the layout of objects in memory is highly compiler-dependent, but the fact remains that the memory layout for an object of type D with A as a nonvirtual base is typically a contiguous series of memory locations, whereas the memory layout for an object of type D with A as a virtual base is typically a contiguous series of memory locations, one of which contains a pointer to an *additional* series of memory locations containing the data members of the virtual base class:

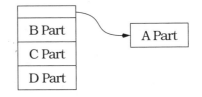

| A Part |
| B Part |
| A Part |
| C Part |
| D Part |

Common memory layout
of a D object where A is a
nonvirtual base class

Common memory layout of
a D object where A is a
virtual base class

(The memory allocated for the virtual base need not be discontiguous with the rest of the memory for the object. That is, in the right-hand diagram above, the memory for the A part of a D object may abut the memory allocated for the B, C, and D parts. Even if that's the case, however, the A part is still typically accessed through a pointer.)

In view of these considerations, it would seem that effective class design in the presence of MI calls for clairvoyance on the part of library designers. Seeing as how run-of-the-mill common sense is an increasingly rare commodity these days, you would be rather ill-advised to rely too heavily on a language feature that calls for designers to be not only anticipatory of future needs, but downright prophetic.

Of course, this could also be said of the choice between virtual and nonvirtual functions in a base class, but there is a crucial difference. Item 36 explains that a virtual function has a well-defined high-level meaning that is distinct from the equally well-defined high-level meaning of a nonvirtual function, so it is possible to choose between the two based on what you want to communicate to writers of subclasses. However, the decision as to whether a base class should be virtual or nonvirtual lacks a well-defined high-level meaning. Rather, that decision is usually based on the structure of the entire inheritance hierarchy, and as such it cannot be made until the entire hierarchy is known. If you need to know exactly how your class is going to be used before you can declare it correctly, it becomes very difficult to design effective classes.

Once you're past the problem of ambiguity and you've settled the question of whether your base class(es) should be virtual, still more complications confront you. Rather than belaboring each of them, I'll simply mention them in passing:

- **Passing constructor arguments to virtual base classes**. Under nonvirtual inheritance, arguments for a base class constructor are specified in the member initialization lists of the classes immediately derived from the base class. Because single inheritance hierarchies need only nonvirtual bases, arguments are passed up the inheritance hierarchy in a very natural fashion: the classes at level n of the hierarchy pass arguments to the classes at level n-1. For constructors of a virtual base class, however, arguments are specified in the member initialization lists of the classes *most derived* from the base. As a result, the class initializing a virtual base may be arbitrarily far from it in the inheritance graph, and furthermore, the class performing the initialization can change as new classes are added to the hierarchy.

- **Dominance of virtual functions**. Just when you thought you had ambiguity all figured out, they change the rules on you. Consider again the diamond-shaped inheritance graph involving classes A, B, C, and D. Suppose that A defines a virtual member function mf, and B redefines it; C and D, however, do not redefine mf. From our earlier discussion, you'd expect this to be ambiguous:

```
D *pd = new D;
pd->mf();                       // A::mf or B::mf?
```

Which mf should be called for a D object, the one directly inherited from B or the one indirectly inherited (via C) from A? The answer is that *it depends on A.* In particular, if A is a nonvirtual base of B or C, then the call is ambiguous, but if A is a virtual base of both B and C, the redefinition of mf in B is said to *dominate* the original definition in A, and the call to mf through pd will resolve (unambiguously) to B::mf. Easy, right?

- **Casting restrictions**. C++ explicitly prohibits you from casting down from a (pointer or reference to a) virtual base class to a derived class. Of course, this prohibition should pose no undue hardships, seeing as how Item 39 describes why you shouldn't be trying to do it in the first place, but it is nonetheless another arbitrary rule to remember.

Perhaps by now you agree that MI can lead to complications. Perhaps you are convinced that no one in their right mind would ever use it. Perhaps you are prepared to propose to the ANSI committee standardizing C++ that multiple inheritance be removed from the language, or at least to propose to your boss that programmers at your site be physically barred from using it. Perhaps, however, you are being too hasty.

Bear in mind that the designer of C++ didn't set out to make multiple inheritance hard to use, it just turned out that making all the pieces work together in a more or less reasonable fashion inherently entailed the introduction of certain complexities. In the above discussion, you may have noticed that the bulk of these complexities arise in conjunction with the use of virtual base classes. If you can avoid the use of virtual bases — that is, if you can avoid the creation of the deadly diamond inheritance graph — things become much more manageable.

For example, Item 34 describes how an *Abstract Base Class* (ABC), also called a *Protocol class*, exists only to specify an interface for derived classes; it typically has no data members, no constructors, a virtual destructor (see Item 14), and a set of pure virtual functions that specify the interface. An ABC for a Person class might look like this:

```
class Person {
public:
  virtual ~Person();

  virtual char * name() const = 0;
  virtual char * birthDate () const = 0;
  virtual char * address() const = 0;
  virtual char * nationality() const = 0;
};
```

Clients of this class must program in terms of Person pointers and references, because abstract classes cannot be instantiated.

To create objects that can be manipulated as `Person` objects, clients of the `Person` Protocol class instantiate concrete subclasses of that class. For example, the `Person` class might have a derived class called `MyPerson`. As a concrete class, `MyPerson` must provide implementations for the pure virtual functions it inherits from `Person`. It could provide these itself, but it might instead choose to use functions that have already been defined for this purpose in another class, a class that exists only to implement the interface specified in an ABC like `Person`. If this special-purpose implementation class is called `Real-Person`, then it's safe to say that the `MyPerson` class *is implemented in terms of* the `RealPerson` class.

An is-implemented-in-terms-of relationship between classes can be represented in two ways: layering (see Item 40) and private inheritance (see Item 41). An example of how to use layering to implement `MyPer-son` in terms of `RealPerson` is provided in Item 34. Here, I demonstrate how to do it using a combination of public and private inheritance.

The basic idea is simple. Because each `MyPerson` object isa `Person`, you know that `MyPerson` must publicly inherit from `Person` (see Item 35). However, because you want to use `RealPerson` as your implementation, you decide to have `MyPerson` privately inherit from `Real-Person`. This establishes the crux of the methodology: combine public inheritance of an interface with private inheritance of an implementation:

```
class String { ... };          // character strings
class Date { ... };            // historical dates
class Address { ... };         // residence addresses
class Country { ... };
class Person { ... };          // as above

class RealPerson {
protected:
  RealPerson(const String& name, const Date& birthday,
            const Address& addr, const Country& country);
  virtual ~RealPerson();

  virtual char * name() const;
  virtual char * birthDate () const;
  virtual char * address() const;
  virtual char * nationality() const;

  ...

};

class MyPerson: public Person, private RealPerson {
public:
  MyPerson(const String& name, const Date& birthday,
          const Address& addr, const Country& country)
  : RealPerson(name, birthday, addr, country) {}
```

```
char * name() const
{ return RealPerson::name(); }

char * birthDate () const
{ return RealPerson::birthDate(); }

char * address() const
{ return RealPerson::address(); }

char * nationality() const
{ return RealPerson::nationality(); }
};
```

Graphically, it looks like this:

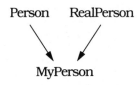

Person   RealPerson

MyPerson

In this example, notice that RealPerson's functions are protected; this reflects the fact that RealPerson is designed specifically to be a base class — it's not expected to stand on its own (see Item 41). To get access to RealPerson's functions, then, MyPerson *must* be a subclass of RealPerson; layering will not do. Like the layering example of Item 34, however, MyPerson itself does no more than translate function interfaces inherited from Person into function implementations inherited from RealPerson. Also similar to layering is the fact that each of MyPerson's functions is characteristically trivial and inline.

This kind of example demonstrates that MI can be both useful and comprehensible, although it's no accident that the dreaded diamond-shaped inheritance graph is conspicuously absent. Still, you must guard against temptation. Sometimes you can fall into the trap of using MI to make a quick fix to an inheritance hierarchy that would be better served by a more fundamental redesign.

For example, suppose you're working with a hierarchy for animated cartoon characters. At least conceptually, it makes sense for any kind of character to dance and sing, but the way in which each type of character performs these activities differs. Furthermore, the default behavior for singing and dancing is to do nothing.

The way to say all that in C++ is like this:

```
class CartoonCharacter {
public:
  virtual void dance() {}
  virtual void sing() {}
};
```

Virtual functions naturally model the constraint that dancing and singing make sense for all CartoonCharacter objects, and do-nothing default behavior is expressed by the empty definitions of those functions in the class (see Item 36).

Suppose that a particular type of cartoon character is a grasshopper, which dances and sings in its own particular way:

```
class Grasshopper: public CartoonCharacter {
public:
  virtual void dance();        // definition is elsewhere
  virtual void sing();         // definition is elsewhere
};
```

Now suppose that after implementing the Grasshopper class, you decide that you also need a class for crickets:

```
class Cricket: public CartoonCharacter {
public:
  virtual void dance();
  virtual void sing();
};
```

As you sit down to implement the Cricket class, you realize that a lot of the code you wrote for the Grasshopper class can be reused. However, it needs to be tweaked a bit here and there to account for the differences in singing and dancing between grasshoppers and crickets. You are suddenly struck by a clever way to reuse your existing code: you'll implement the Cricket class *in terms of* the Grasshopper class, and you'll use virtual functions to allow the Cricket class to customize Grasshopper behavior!

You immediately recognize that the twin requirements — an is-implemented-in-terms-of relationship and the ability to redefine virtual functions — mean that Cricket will have to privately inherit from Grasshopper (see Item 41), but of course a cricket is still a cartoon character, so you redeclare Cricket to inherit from both Grasshopper and CartoonCharacter:

```
class Cricket:public CartoonCharacter,
              private Grasshopper {
public:
  virtual void dance();
  virtual void sing();
};
```

You then set out to make the necessary modifications to the Grasshopper class. In particular, you need to declare some new virtual functions for Cricket to redefine:

```
class Grasshopper: public CartoonCharacter {
public:
  virtual void dance();
  virtual void sing();

protected:
  virtual void danceCustomization1();
  virtual void danceCustomization2();

  virtual void singCustomization();
};
```

Dancing for grasshoppers is now defined like this:

```
void Grasshopper::dance()
{
  perform common dancing actions;

  danceCustomization1();

  perform more common dancing actions;

  danceCustomization2();

  perform final common dancing actions;
}
```

Grasshopper singing is orchestrated similarly.

Clearly, the Cricket class must be updated to take into account the new virtual functions it must redefine:

```
class Cricket: public CartoonCharacter,
               private Grasshopper {
public:
  virtual void dance() { Grasshopper::dance(); }
  virtual void sing() { Grasshopper::sing(); }

protected:
  virtual void danceCustomization1();
  virtual void danceCustomization2();

  virtual void singCustomization();
};
```

This seems to work fine. When a Cricket object is told to dance, it will execute the common dance code in the Grasshopper class, then execute the dance customization code in the Cricket class, then continue with the code in Grasshopper::dance, etc.

There is a serious flaw in your design, however, and that is that you have run headlong into Occam's razor, a bad idea with a razor of any kind, and especially so when it belongs to William of Occam. Occamism preaches that entities should not be multiplied beyond necessity, and in this case the entities in question are inheritance relationships.

If you believe that multiple inheritance is more complicated than single inheritance (and I hope that you do), then the design of the `Cricket` class is needlessly complex.

Fundamentally, the problem is that it is *not* true that the `Cricket` class is-implemented-in-terms-of the `Grasshopper` class. Rather, the `Cricket` class and the `Grasshopper` class *share common code*. In particular, they share the code that determines the dancing and singing behavior that grasshoppers and crickets have in common.

The way to say that two classes have something in common is *not* to have one class inherit from the other, but to have *both* of them inherit from a common base class. The common code for grasshoppers and crickets doesn't belong in the `Grasshopper` class, nor does it belong in the `Cricket` class; it belongs in a new class from which they both inherit, say, `Insect`:

```
class CartoonCharacter { ... };

class Insect: public CartoonCharacter {
public:
  virtual void dance();          // common code for both
  virtual void sing();           // grasshoppers and crickets

protected:
  virtual void danceCustomization1();
  virtual void danceCustomization2();

  virtual void singCustomization();
};

class Grasshopper: public Insect {
protected:
  virtual void danceCustomization1();
  virtual void danceCustomization2();

  virtual void singCustomization();
};

class Cricket: public Insect {
protected:
  virtual void danceCustomization1();
  virtual void danceCustomization2();

  virtual void singCustomization();
};
```

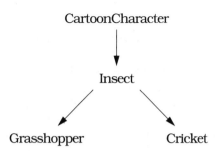

Notice how much cleaner this design is. Only single inheritance is involved, and furthermore, only *public* inheritance is used. The fact that both Grasshopper and Cricket are specializations of Insect is directly expressed by the fact that the only functions in those classes specialize the common behavior they inherit from their base class. In particular, Grasshopper and Cricket define only customization functions; they inherit the dance and sing functions unchanged from Insect. William of Occam would be proud.

Interestingly, although this design is cleaner than the one involving MI, it may initially have appeared to be dirtier. After all, compared to the MI approach, this single-inheritance architecture calls for the introduction of a brand new class, a class that is unnecessary if MI is used. Why introduce an extra class if you don't have to?

This brings you face to face with the seductive nature of multiple inheritance. On the surface, MI seems to be the easier course of action. It adds no new classes, and though it calls for the addition of some new virtual functions to the Grasshopper class, those functions have to be added somewhere in any case.

Imagine now a programmer maintaining a large C++ class library, one in which a new class has to be added, much as the Cricket class had to be added to the existing CartoonCharacter/Grasshopper hierarchy. The programmer knows that a large number of clients use the existing hierarchy, so the bigger the change to the library, the greater the disruption to clients. The programmer is determined to minimize that kind of disruption. Mulling over the options, the programmer realizes that if a single private inheritance link from Grasshopper to Cricket is added, no other change to the hierarchy will be needed. The programmer smiles at the thought, pleased with the prospect of a large increase in functionality at the cost of only a slight increase in complexity.

Imagine now that that maintenance programmer is you. Resist the seduction.

44 Say what you mean; understand what you're saying.

In the introduction to this section on inheritance and object-oriented design, I emphasized the importance of understanding what different object-oriented constructs in C++ *mean*. This is quite different from just knowing the rules of the language. For example, the rules of C++ say that if class B publicly inherits from class A, there is a standard conversion from a B pointer to an A pointer; that the public member functions of A are inherited as public member functions of B, etc. That's all true, but it's close to useless if you're trying to translate your software design into C++. Instead, you need to understand that public inheritance means isa, that if B publicly inherits from A, every object of type B isa object of type A, too. Thus, if you mean isa in your design, you know you have to use public inheritance.

Saying what you mean is only half the battle. The flip side of the coin is understanding what you're saying, and it's just as important. For example, it's irresponsible, if not downright immoral, to run around declaring member functions nonvirtual without recognizing that in so doing you are imposing constraints on subclasses. In declaring a nonvirtual member function, what you're really saying is that the function represents an invariant over specialization, and it would be disastrous if you didn't know that.

The equivalence of public inheritance and isa, and of nonvirtual member functions and invariance over specialization, are examples of how certain C++ constructs correspond to design-level ideas. The list below summarizes the most important of these mappings.

- **A common base class means common traits**. If class B and class C both declare class A as a base, then B and C inherit common data members and/or common member functions from A. See Item 43.

- **Public inheritance means isa**. If class B publicly inherits from class A, then every object of type B is also an object of type A, but not vice versa. See Item 35.

- **Private inheritance means is-implemented-in-terms-of**. If class B privately inherits from class A, then objects of type B are simply implemented in terms of objects of type A; no design-level conceptual relationship exists between objects of types A and B. See Item 41.

- **Layering means has-a or is-implemented-in-terms-of**. If class A contains a data member of type B, then objects of type A either have a component of type B or are implemented in terms of objects of type B. See Item 40.

The following mappings apply only when public inheritance is involved:

- **A pure virtual function means that function interface only is inherited**. If a class A declares a pure virtual member function mf, then subclasses of A must inherit the interface for mf and must supply their own implementations for it. See Item 36.

- **A simple virtual function means that function interface plus a default implementation is inherited**. If a class A declares a simple (not pure) virtual function mf, then subclasses of A must inherit the interface for mf, but they may also inherit a default implementation, if they choose. See Item 36.

- **A nonvirtual function means that function interface plus a mandatory implementation is inherited**. If a class A declares a nonvirtual member function mf, then subclasses of A must inherit both the interface for mf and its implementation. In effect, mf defines an invariant over specialization of A. See Item 36.

Miscellany

Some guidelines for effective C++ programming simply defy convenient categorization. This section is where such guidelines come to roost. Not that that diminishes their importance. If you are to write effective software, you must understand what the compiler is doing for you (to you?) behind your back, how to ensure that global objects are initialized before they are used, what features will soon be creeping into your C++ compiler, and where to go for authoritative answers on what's in the language and what's not. In this final section of the book, I expound on these issues, and more.

45 Know what functions C++ silently writes and calls.

When is an empty class not an empty class? When C++ gets through with it. In general, if you don't write them yourself, your thoughtful compiler will write its own versions of a copy constructor, an assignment operator, and a pair of address-of operators. Furthermore, if you don't declare any constructors, it will write a default constructor for you, too. All these functions will be public. In other words, if you write this,

```
class Empty{};
```

you may end up with this:

```
class Empty {
public:
  Empty();                      // default constructor
  Empty(const Empty& rhs);      // copy constructor

  Empty&
  operator=(const Empty& rhs);  // assignment operator

  Empty* operator&();           // address-of operators
  const Empty* operator&() const;
};
```

If `Empty` were derived from some other class, and that other class had a destructor, C++ would also write a destructor for `Empty`, a topic I'll return to below.

Now in fact these functions are generated only if they are needed, but it doesn't take much to need them. The following code will cause each function to be generated:

```
const Empty e1;              // default constructor
Empty e2 = e1;               // copy constructor
e2 = e1;                     // assignment operator

Empty *pe2 = &e2;            // address-of
                             // operator (non-const)

const Empty *pe1 = &e1;      // address-of
                             // operator (const)
```

Given that the compiler is writing functions for you, what do the functions do? Well, the default constructor does nothing — it just enables you to define objects of the class, and the default address-of operators just return the address of the object. These three functions are effectively defined like this:

```
inline Empty::Empty(){}

inline Empty * Empty::operator&() { return this; }

inline const Empty * Empty::operator&() const
{ return this; }
```

As for the copy constructor and the assignment operator, the official rule is this: the default copy constructor (assignment operator) performs memberwise copy construction (assignment) of the nonstatic data members of the class. That is, if m is a nonstatic data member of type T in a class C, and C declares no copy constructor (assignment operator), then m will be copy constructed (assigned) using the copy constructor (assignment operator) defined for T, if there is one. If there isn't, the rule will be recursively applied to m's data members until a copy constructor (assignment operator) or built-in type (e.g., int, double, pointer, etc.) is found. By default, objects of built-in types are copy constructed (assigned) using bitwise copy from the source object to the destination object. For classes that inherit from other classes, these rules for default copy construction and assignment are applied to each level of the inheritance hierarchy, so user-defined copy constructors and assignment operators are called at whatever level they are declared.

What? Okay, let's take a look at an example. Consider the declaration of a `NamedInt` class, a class that allows you to associate names with integers. The name of the integer will be stored as a `String` object, so things might look something like this:

```
class String {
public:
  String(const char *value = 0);
  String(const String& rhs);
  String& operator=(const String& rhs);

  ...

};
class NamedInt {
private:
  String nameValue;
  int intValue;

public:
  NamedInt(char *name, int value);
  NamedInt(const String& name, int value);

  ...

};
```

Because the NamedInt class declares at least one constructor, the compiler won't generate a default constructor, but because the class fails to declare a copy constructor or an assignment operator, the compiler will generate those functions (if they are needed). Consider the following call to the copy constructor:

```
NamedInt i("Smallest Prime Number", 2);

NamedInt j = i;                   // calls copy constructor
```

The copy constructor generated by the compiler must initialize j.nameValue and j.intValue using i.nameValue and i.intValue, respectively. The type of NamedInt::nameValue is String, and String has a copy constructor defined, so j.nameValue will be initialized by calling the String copy constructor with i.nameValue as its argument. On the other hand, the type of NamedInt::intValue is int, and no copy constructor is defined for ints, so j.intValue will be initialized by copying the bits over from i.intValue. The compiler-generated assignment operator for NamedInt would behave the same way.

For a discussion of the often-overlooked interactions between pointer members and the compiler-generated copy constructor and assignment operator, check out Item 11.

There is one additional case where the compiler will generate a function for you. If you derive a class from another class, and that other class has a destructor, C++ will generate a public, nonvirtual destructor for you (see also Item 14):

```
class B {
public:
  ~B();
};

class D: public B {};          // D::~D is implicitly
                               // generated
```

Like the implicitly generated default constructor, the generated default destructor is effectively a no-op.

All this gives rise to the question, what do you do if you want to disallow use of these functions? That is, what if you deliberately don't declare, for example, an `operator=` because you never *ever* want to allow assignment of objects in your class? The solution to that little teaser is the subject of Item 27.

46 Prefer compile-time and link-time errors to runtime errors.

As defined in the ARM (see Item 50), there is no such thing as a mandatory runtime error in C++. No detection of division by zero, no checking for array bounds violations, nothing of that kind. Once your program gets through the compiler and linker, you're on your own — there's no safety net. Much like skydiving, some people are exhilarated by this state of affairs, others are paralyzed with fear. The motivation behind the philosophy, of course, is efficiency: without runtime checks, programs are smaller and run faster.

There is a different way to approach things. Languages like Smalltalk and LISP generally detect fewer kinds of errors during compilation and linking, but provide hefty runtime systems that catch errors during execution. Unlike C++, these languages are almost always interpreted, and you pay a performance penalty for the extra flexibility they offer.

Never forget that you are programming in C++. Even if you find the Smalltalk/LISP philosophy appealing, put it out of your mind. There's a lot to be said for adhering to the party line, and in this case that means eschewing runtime errors. Whenever you can, push the detection of an error back from runtime to link-time, or, ideally, to compile-time.

Such a methodology pays dividends not only in terms of program size and speed, but also in terms of reliability. If your program gets through the compiler and the linker without eliciting any error messages, you know that there aren't any compiler- or linker-detectable errors in your program, period. (The other possibility, of course, is that there are bugs in your compiler and/or linker, but let's not depress ourselves by admitting to such possibilities.)

With runtime errors, the situation is very different. Just because your program doesn't generate any runtime errors during a particular run, how can you be sure that it won't generate any errors during a different run, when you do things in a different order, use different data, or run for a longer or shorter period of time? You can test your program until you're blue in the face, but you'll still never cover all the possibilities. As a result, detecting errors at runtime is simply less secure than is catching them during compilation or linking.

Often, by making relatively minor changes to your design, you can catch during compilation what might otherwise be a runtime error. This frequently involves the addition of new types to the program. For example, suppose that you are writing a class to represent dates in time. Your first cut might look like this:

```
class Date {
public:
  Date(short day, short month, long year);

  ...

};
```

If you were to implement this constructor, one of the problems you'd face would be that of sanity checking on the values for the day and the month. Let's see how you can eliminate the need to validate the value passed in for the month.

One obvious approach is to employ an enumerated type instead of an integer:

```
enum Month { Jan, Feb, Mar, ... , Nov, Dec };

class Date {
public:
  Date(short day, Month month, long year);

  ...

};
```

Unfortunately, this doesn't buy you that much, because enums don't have to be initialized:

```
Month m;
Date d1(22, m, 1857);           // m is undefined
```

As a result, the Date constructor would still have to validate the value of the month parameter.

To achieve enough security to dispense with runtime checks, you've got to use a class to represent months, and you must ensure that only valid months are created:

```
class Date {
public:

  class Month {
  friend class Date;

  private:
    const unsigned short monthNumber;
    Month(short number): monthNumber(number) {}
  };

  Date(short day, Month month, long year);

  static const Month Jan, Feb, ..., Nov, Dec;
};

const Date::Month Date::Jan(1);
const Date::Month Date::Feb(2);
...
const Date::Month Date::Nov(11);
const Date::Month Date::Dec(12);
```

Here I've used nested classes (see Item 49), but the same approach works even if the classes aren't nested. If your compiler doesn't support nested classes yet, take a look at Item 42 for a description of how you can approximate them.

A number of features in this example combine to make it work correctly. First, the Month constructor is private. This prevents clients from creating new month objects; the only Month objects available are the static ones contained inside the Date class. Second, the Date class is a friend of the Month class, so it has access to the private Month constructor, hence it can construct the static Month objects. Third, each Month object is const, so it can't be changed (otherwise the temptation to transform January into June might prove overwhelming from time to time). Finally, because the Month objects may be used anywhere and anytime, you've got to take precautions to ensure that they are initialized before they are used (see Item 47).

Given these classes, it is impossible for a client to specify an invalid month, and the Date constructor can therefore dispense with sanity checking on that parameter. On the other hand, the constructor must still check the day parameter for validity — how many days hath September, April, June, and November?

A final point: because the Month objects are statics inside Date, a date must be declared like this:

```
Date d(22, Date::Apr, 1857);   // month name is fully
                               // qualified
```

This is ugly, but this ugliness can be hidden by the clever use of global references (see Item 28):

```
const Date::Month& Jan = Date::Jan;
const Date::Month& Feb = Date::Feb;
...
const Date::Month& Dec = Date::Dec;

const Date d(22, Apr, 1857);
```

This `Date` example replaces runtime checks with compile-time checks. You may be wondering when it is possible to use link-time checks. In truth, not very often. C++ uses the linker to ensure that needed functions are defined exactly once (see Item 45 for a description of what it takes to "need" a function), and it also uses the linker to ensure that global objects (including static class data members) are defined exactly once. You'll tend to use the linker in the same way. For example, Item 27 describes why it can be useful to deliberately avoid defining a function you declare explicitly.

Now don't get carried away. It's impractical to eliminate the need for *all* runtime checking. Any program that accepts interactive input, for example, is likely to have to validate that input. Similarly, a class implementing arrays that perform bounds checking (see Item 18) is usually going to have to validate the array index against the bounds every time an array access is made. Nonetheless, shifting checks from runtime to compile- or link-time is always a worthwhile goal, and you should pursue that goal whenever it is practical. Your reward for doing so is programs that are smaller, faster, and substantially more reliable.

47 Ensure that global objects are initialized before they're used.

Listen, you're an adult now, so you can take care of yourself. That means you don't need me to tell you that it's foolhardy to access the value of an object that hasn't been initialized. In fact, the whole notion may strike you as absurd; constructors make sure that objects are always properly initialized when they're declared, *n'est-ce pas*?

Well, yes and no. Within a particular translation unit (i.e., source file), everything works fine, but what do you do when the initialization of an object in one translation unit depends on the value of another object in a different translation unit, and that second object itself requires initialization?

Here's an example:

```
#include <iostream.h>

int f()
{
  int input;
  cin >> input;                    // cin is a global object
  return input;
}

int i = f();                       // i is also at
                                   // global scope

main()
{
  cout << "The value of i is " << i << '\n';
}
```

The global integer i must be initialized by calling the function f. Inside f, the global object cin is used. (You can find the declarations for cin, cout, etc., in <iostream.h>.) If cin isn't initialized before f is called, disaster will ensue, because you'll attempt to read from an uninitialized stream. In view of the fact that both cin and i are global, how can you be sure that i won't be initialized before cin is?

This issue arises whenever you need to worry about the initialization order of what I call *global objects*: static class data members and objects at global scope. Global objects share the characteristic that they are *conceptually* initialized prior to execution of main, although in fact some of the initializations may be delayed until after that time, as described below. In addition to the common use of the global streams cin and cout, an example of the use of global objects to represent the months of the year is described in Item 46.

You know only three things about the initialization of global objects:

- All the global objects in a translation unit will be initialized before the first use of any function or object defined in that translation unit.

- If global object A is defined before global object B in the same translation unit, then A will be initialized before B.

- Any global object that is not explicitly initialized in a translation unit is implicitly initialized to 0 by the compiler. Implicit initializations of this type are performed before any explicit initializations.

Notice that there is absolutely no mention of any initialization order *between* translation units. However, it turns out that you have enough information here to force the compiler to initialize global objects before they are used.

The gist of the trick is this:

1. For each set of global objects of type G that you want to explicitly initialize, you declare a class GI with a static integer count, a constructor and a destructor. The count field is used to keep track of the total number of GI objects that currently exist, the GI constructor is used to effectively construct the global objects of type G, and the GI destructor is used to effectively destruct them. Typically, GI is a friend of G.

2. At the bottom of the header file that declares the existence of the global objects of type G, declare a file static object of class GI.

3. In the GI constructor, initialize the global G objects if and only if count is zero, then increment count. In the GI destructor, decrement count and, if it is now zero, clean up after the global objects of type G.

Let's see how these pieces work together in the example above to ensure that cin is initialized prior to calling f to initialize i.

There are three files of concern here. One is your good friend <iostream.h>. The second is the implementation file for iostreams, which I'll call iostream.cc. The final one is the file containing the definition of i, which I'll call yourFile.cc (or, as they say in the DOS world, YOURFILE.CC).

The relevant part of <iostream.h> looks something like this:

```
class istream_withassign
{ ... };                        // cin's class

extern istream_withassign cin;  // declaration of cin

// class to be used to effectively construct and destruct
// objects of type istream_withassign
class Iostream_init {
private:
  static unsigned short count;  // number of Iostream_init
                                // objects currently in
                                // existence
public:
  Iostream_init();
  ~Iostream_init();
};

static
Iostream_init iostream_init;    // static object at bottom
                                // of .h file
```

Now don't get all upset if your version of <iostream.h> doesn't look exactly like this — the idea is the important thing. In terms of the dis-

cussion above, G is `istream_withassign`, GI is `Iostream_init`, and
cin is the global object you want to initialize before it's used.

Here's `yourFile.cc`:

```
#include <iostream.h>

int f()
{
  int input;
  cin >> input;
  return input;
}

int i = f();

main()
{
  cout << "The value of i is " << i << '\n';
}
```

The important thing to recognize is that by including `<iostream.h>` at
the top of `yourFile.cc`, you have implicitly declared a static object,
`iostream_init`, before anything else in the file. In particular,
`iostream_init` is declared *before* i. That means that `iostream_init`
must be initialized before i, because they are both in the same translation unit. From above, you know that `iostream_init` has a constructor, and you know that that constructor will be used to effectively
construct cin. So by the time i is initialized, you're guaranteed that
cin has already been initialized.

This sets the stage for `iostream.cc`:

```
#include <iostream.h>

istream_withassign cin;          // definition of cin

unsigned short
Iostream_init::count;            // definition of
                                 // Iostream_init::count

Iostream_init::Iostream_init()
{
  if (count++ == 0) {
    do whatever is necessary to effectively construct cin;
  }
}

Iostream_init::~Iostream_init()
{
  if (--count == 0) {
    do whatever is necessary to effectively destruct cin;
  }
}
```

This is all pretty straightforward, and it should be fairly clear what will happen. Each file including `<iostream.h>` implicitly declares an object of type `Iostream_init`, and the constructor for that object effectively constructs `cin`, being careful not to initialize it more than once. Similarly, at the end of the program, each `Iostream_init` object will be destroyed, and the last one that is destroyed will also effectively destruct `cin`.

Perhaps the only odd-looking construct in `iostream.cc` is the definition of `Iostream_init::count` without an initialization. The definition is required by the language — all global objects must be defined exactly once — but you want to rely on the default initialization of a static object to 0, hence the lack of an initialization.

Maybe you're wondering why I keep saying that the `Iostream_init` constructor "effectively" constructs `cin`, and the `Iostream_init` destructor "effectively" destructs it. That's because most global objects requiring this kind of initialization are of classes that *do* have constructors and destructors, and these objects are of course officially constructed and destructed whenever the compiler gets around to doing it. You'll recall that you don't know precisely when these functions will be called, and that's why you have to go to all the trouble described above in the first place. Nonetheless, `cin`'s constructor and destructor will most certainly be called, and to accommodate that fact you need to add a caveat to the steps above:

4. Ensure that the constructor and destructor for G do not interfere with any of the work done in GI's constructor and destructor, respectively.

This is hardly a minor consideration. It's often just as disastrous for an object to be constructed or destructed more than once as it is for the construction or destruction not to take place at all. Remember also that by the time a global object's constructor is called, that object may already have been used, so it may no longer be in the same state it was in when it was effectively constructed. Similarly, after a global object's destructor is called, that object may still be used until it is effectively destructed.

Clearly there's no magic here that can't be circumvented. For any given translation unit, the global objects will be initialized in top-to-bottom order, so if you set things up such that global object A must be initialized before global object B, and you also make A's initialization dependent on B's having already been initialized, you are just asking for trouble. If you steer shy of such pathological situations, however, the scheme described in this item should serve you quite nicely.

48 Pay attention to compiler warnings.

Many programmers routinely ignore compiler warnings. After all, if the problem were really serious, it'd be an error, right? This kind of thinking may be relatively harmless in other languages, but in C++ you're better off banking on the compiler writer having a better grasp of what's going on than you do. For example, here's an error that everybody makes at one time or another:

```
class A {
public:
  virtual void f() const;
};

class B: public A {
public:
  virtual void f();
};
```

The idea is for `B::f` to redefine the virtual function `A::f`, but there's a mistake: in `A`, `f` is a `const` member function, but in `B` it's not declared `const`. One popular compiler I know says this about that:

```
warning: B::f() hides virtual A::f()
```

Too many inexperienced programmers respond to this message by saying to themselves, "Of *course* `B::f` hides `A::f` — that's what it's *supposed* to do!" Wrong. What the compiler is trying to tell you is that the `f` declared in `A` has not been redeclared in `B`, it's been hidden entirely (see Item 50 for a description of why this is so). Ignoring this compiler warning will almost certainly lead to erroneous program behavior, followed by a lot of debugging to find out about something that the compiler detected in the first place.

After you gain experience with the warning messages from a particular compiler, of course, you'll learn to understand what the different messages mean (which is often very different from what they *seem* to mean, alas). Once you have that experience, there may be a whole range of warnings you'll choose to ignore. That's fine, but it's important to make sure that before you dismiss a warning, you understand exactly what it's trying to tell you.

As long as we're on the topic of warnings, recall that warnings are inherently implementation-dependent, so it's not a good idea to get sloppy in your programming, relying on the compiler to spot your mistakes for you. The function-shadowing code above, for instance, goes through a different (but commonly used) compiler with nary a squawk. Compilers are supposed to translate C++ into an executable format, not act as your personal safety net. You want that kind of safety? Program in Ada.

49 Plan for coming language features.

You say you like C++ now, but you want *more*? No problem. Depending on the compiler you're using, you have as many as three exciting new features to look forward to, each just *guaranteed* to make your life even more fulfilling than it already is.

The features in question are nested types, templates, and exceptions. None of these is present in a release 2.0 compiler; a compiler compatible with release 2.1 supports nested types; and a compiler at release level 3.0 offers both nested types and templates. For the time being, exceptions are available only in experimental and/or proprietary compilers.

In this item, I offer a brief description of each of these features. For the full story, consult a comprehensive C++ textbook or turn to the ARM (see Item 50).

The idea behind nested types is simply this: types declared inside a class (or a struct) should behave like members of the class, being scoped as usual and obeying the public, protected, and private access restrictions. Types that are defined only for the purpose of implementing a class should be hidden from general view, and types that are for general use but that are associated with a particular class should be declared within the class, thus avoiding "pollution of the global namespace" (see Item 28).

For example, if you wanted to write a class to represent a set of objects of type T, and you wanted to use a linked list data structure to implement the set, the type of the structures in the linked list would be nobody's business but your own, and you could express that fact this way:

```
class Set {
private:
  // structures to be linked together
  struct Item {
    T data;                      // data item in the set
    Item *next;                  // ptr to next list struct
    Item(const T& newItem);      // ctor for Item struct
  };
```

```
      Item *headOfList;              // ptr to head of
                                     // linked list
  public:
    Set();
    ~Set();

    ...

  };

  Set s;                            // fine

  Item *itemPtr;                    // error! — Item is
                                    // called Set::Item

  Set::Item *itemPtr;               // error! — Set::Item is
                                    // private
```

Items 28 and 46 provide other examples of how nested types might be used, and Item 42 describes how nested classes and structs can be approximated with a compiler that doesn't directly support them.

Speaking of the Set class, note that the code for the class is the same regardless of the type of objects stored in the set — the only thing that changes is the type of those objects, T. This is a situation that just *begs* for the use of templates, because templates are the C++ mechanism for parameterizing a class or function on the basis of type.

To apply templates to the Set class, all you have to do is specify that the class is to be generated from a template and that the template takes as a parameter a type name you call T:

```
  // Set is a template class taking a type parameter T
  template<class T>
  class Set {
  private:
    struct Item {
      T data;                       // note use of type param
      Item *next;

      Item(const T& newItem);       // ditto
    };

    Item *headOfList;

  public:

    ...                             // same as before

  };
```

Don't be fooled by the use of the word "class" in the template declaration. T can be any type specification; it's not limited to being the name of a class.

When you declare an object of type Set, you must provide the type parameter required by the template:

```
Set<double> doubleSet;          // a set of doubles
Set<char *> stringSet;          // a set of char pointers
Set< Set<int> > intSetSet;      // a set of sets of ints
```

Templates can be used to specify functions as well as classes (see Item 1), can take more than one parameter, and can take non-type parameters. For example, if you wanted to specify a template for fixed-size buffers of different types of objects, you might do it this way:

```
template<class T, int size>
class Buffer {
private:
  T buffer[size];               // private array of size
                                // elements, each a T
                                // object

  ...

};

Buffer<int, 128> intBuf;        // a buffer of 128 ints

Buffer< Set<int>, 1000>
  intSetBuf;                    // a buffer of 1000
                                // sets of ints
```

There's more to templates than is shown here, but this should be enough to whet your appetite. For an idea of how to simulate templates using the preprocessor (useful for tiding you over until your compiler supports templates), see Item 1. For a discussion of the relationship between templates and inheritance, see Item 42. By the way, template is a reserved word.

The final preview of coming attractions concerns C++'s impending support for exceptions. The basic idea behind exception handling is this: when a condition arises that the current code can't handle, it *throws* an exception. That exception is *caught* by the block most recently entered that has declared a willingness to handle exceptions of the type that is thrown. Only special blocks called *try blocks* can catch exceptions. The keywords try, throw, and catch are all reserved.

Once an exception has been thrown, control transfers to the place where it is caught, and there is no returning to the location of the exception. This is known as non-resumptive exception handling.

Here's an example based on the template class for statically allocated buffers you just saw, except that this time the memory is dynamically allocated:

```
template<class T>
class DynamicBuffer {
private:
  T *bufferPointer;

public:
  DynamicBuffer(int size) throw (const char*);

  ~DynamicBuffer() { delete [] bufferPointer; }

  ...

};
```

Everything here looks pretty normal, except that the constructor has an additional *exception specification* that indicates that it may throw exceptions of type const char*. The way it might do that becomes evident when you examine the definition of the constructor:

```
template<class T>
DynamicBuffer<T>::DynamicBuffer(int size)throw (const char*)
{
  // try to allocate memory
  bufferPointer = new T[size];

  // check to see if allocation succeeded; if not,
  // throw an exception
  if (bufferPointer == 0)
    throw "Out of Memory";
}
```

Don't get sidetracked by all the template declaration gobbledegook at the beginning of this function. This constructor just calls new to allocate the requested memory, and, if new returns 0, the constructor throws an exception, in this case the character string "Out of Memory".

When such an exception is thrown, the C++ runtime system will search for the block most recently entered that can catch an exception of this type. Only try blocks can catch exceptions, and *catch blocks* are attached to try blocks. For example:

```
main()
{
  try {
    DynamicBuffer<long> buffer(50000);

    ...

  }
  catch (const char *string) {
    cerr << "Exception raised: " << string << '\n';
    abort();
  }
}
```

Inside `main`, you want to allocate a big dynamic buffer and then do some work with it, but you also want to be able to catch exceptions of type `const char*` should they arise during the course of your work, so you enclose your work with `buffer` inside a try block. To this try block you attach a catch block for exceptions of type `const char*`, which you handle (not particularly imaginatively) by printing out the exception parameter and then calling `abort`.

None of this may strike you as all that big a deal. "After all, what's wrong with `setjmp` and `longjmp`?," I hear you mutter. Destructors, that's what. Consider a slightly revised version of `main`:

```
main()
{
  try {
    DynamicBuffer<char> buf1(128);
    DynamicBuffer< Set<int> > buf2(1024);
    DynamicBuffer<long> buf3(50000);

    ...

  }
  catch (const char* string) {
    cerr << "Exception raised: " << string << '\n';
    abort();
  }
}
```

Suppose that the constructors for `buf1` and `buf2` execute successfully, but then the constructor for `buf3` throws an exception. Control will transfer to the catch block as before, but what should happen to `buf1` and `buf2`? They were constructed inside the try block, but control has now left that block, never to return. When should their destructors be called? Following the usual practice of C++, their destructors should be called when control exits the try block, but clearly no destructor should be invoked for `buf3`, because it wasn't ever constructed. Suddenly things are no longer quite as simple as they once seemed.

This question — that of which destructors should be called when an exception is thrown — is the fundamental reason why correct exception handling can't be left to programmers to implement on their own; core language support is absolutely essential. Furthermore, the more you think about the matter, the more complicated it becomes. For example, how many destructors should be called if an exception is thrown while an array of objects is being constructed, and only some of the objects in the array were constructed? What if an exception is thrown during the construction of an object that inherits from other classes, and that object has successfully constructed its base class parts but not its derived class parts? On and on it goes; just thinking about it makes my head hurt.

This is only the briefest introduction to exception handling in C++; there's much more you must know before you can use it effectively. Some of the important details include a description of how exception specifications for functions interact with type checking, what happens when a function throws an exception that's not in its exception specification, what happens when an exception is thrown but is never caught, what occurs when a catch block itself throws an exception, and how the objects that are thrown during an exception can be used in a catch block.

When it becomes commonly available, exception handling will be an invaluable addition to the language, but EH (as it's known in the chicest of C++ circles) is not yet supported by most compilers. Unfortunately, the need to handle exceptional conditions stubbornly refuses to go away until EH is available, so it's worth a quick sketch of possible strategies for dealing with runtime traumas. What follows is enough to give you a flavor for the different approaches that are possible, but is hardly a comprehensive description of all the ins and outs of each methodology:

- **Call a global error-handling function**. Not very flexible, but easy to implement, and it makes it fairly easy to identify likely throw locations when you decide to go back and add real EH to existing software. Needless to say, clients should be allowed to specify the error-handling function to call. This is the strategy currently employed by the default operator new (see Item 7).

- **Call a class-specific error-handling function**. More flexible than using a global function and more object-oriented, too, but a bit more work. Item 7 gives an example of how it can be implemented, and Item 24 shows how it could be used.

- **Include a status field in each object**. This field is set to some "valid" value at the end of a constructor and is set to some appropriate "invalid" value if the object is corrupted, such as when a member function encounters an exceptional condition. Each member function of the class checks to ensure that this->status is valid before doing anything; if it's not, the function simply returns immediately (producing undefined results). Included in the class interface is a function that returns the status of an object, so it's possible for clients to query the current state of an object to see if the object is valid.

This approach is currently employed in many implementations of the iostream library, where streams that have become corrupt in some way (e.g., due to an attempt to write to a file when the disk is full) simply ignore all subsequent calls to their member functions.

- **Have functions return a status value**. If each function returns a status value, it becomes possible for callers to detect when an error has occurred. Furthermore, status values can be customized on a per-function basis to indicate precisely what has gone wrong. Unfortunately, the only practical way to return such a status value is through an extra parameter passed to the function by reference, because many functions need their return value for conveying useful information and others — notably constructors — have no return value at all. (Okay, okay, you could also use a global variable, but how un-object-oriented do you want to be? If you're going to do that, why not just use BASIC?) With this technique, conscientious error detection requires that callers follow each function call with a conditional,

```
f(x, y, status);          // call function
if (!status)              // check status
  handle the exceptional condition;
```

and experience has shown that clients almost always find this extra-parameter approach more trouble than it's worth.

- **Maintain your own stack of destructible objects**. If you're working on an application that absolutely positively needs to have exception handling and needs to have it *now*, you can approximate the behavior of the upcoming EH mechanism. You accomplish this by explicitly maintaining your own stack of objects that should be destructed if an exception is thrown. Your stack shadows the runtime stack, pushing objects on the stack as they are created, popping them off as they are destructed.

To implement this scheme, you need three additional classes: one for objects whose destructors must be called if an exception is thrown, one for exception handlers, and one for exceptions:

```
// class for "mandatorily destructable objects"
class MDObjects { ... };

class ExceptionHandler { ... };

class Exception {
public:
  void Throw();

  ...

};
```

When a new `ExceptionHandler` object is defined, an entry is made into the shadow stack and `setjmp` is called to save the environment. Similarly, when an object that inherits from class `MDObjects` is created, it is placed on the shadow stack. Because the determination of whether the objects of a class should always be destructed upon an exception is usually independent of the other characteristics of the class, this usually involves multiple inheritance *with* virtual base classes (see Item 43), a sure sign that things are getting complicated. Finally, when an `Exception` object is thrown, the objects on the top of the shadow stack are destructed and removed until an `ExceptionHandler` object is found that can handle the exception. Then a `longjmp` is made to the point associated with the handler.

- **Use raw `setjmp` and `longjmp` and hope for the best**. Damn the destructors, full speed ahead! This is the teenage sex approach: fast, easy, and dangerous.

Given that many compilers don't yet support nested types, templates, or exceptions, you might wonder why you should even worry about these features. The answer, quite simply, is that you should always be designing your software with an eye toward the future. By knowing that nested classes will soon be ubiquitous, you gain insight into how you can avoid polluting the global namespace (see Item 28), and you can design your current classes with nesting in mind, perhaps by naming them in such a way that you can automate the process of retroactively nesting them when your compiler supports it. If you are aware that templates are just around the corner, you can more easily avoid the error of improperly using inheritance (see Item 42), and you can get some experience with templates by simulating them with the preprocessor (see Item 1). Finally, by keeping exception handling in mind, you can write your code with an eye toward identifying exceptional conditions and determining how they should be handled, and you can employ stopgap measures until true exception handling becomes available to you.

50 Read the ARM.

The ARM is a book: *The Annotated C++ Reference Manual*, by Margaret A. Ellis and Bjarne Stroustrup (Addison-Wesley, 1990). For programmers who are not keeping up with the deliberations of the committee wrestling to come up with an ANSI standard for C++ (a standard that's not expected until at least 1993), the ARM is the most accessible final authority on what is and isn't in the language, and on how what's in is supposed to behave. The ARM is just what it says — a reference manual. It is *not* a book for people who want to learn the language from scratch.

Not only does the ARM tell you most anything you are ever likely to want to know about the finer points of C++ (though not about the libraries — see Item 2), it also helps you tell the difference between bugs in your code and bugs in your compiler. For example, you notice that sizeof never returns 0 for a class, not even for a class with nothing in it. Bug? (No — see ARM section 5.3.2.) You want to know whether it is safe to delete a pointer that's already been deleted or that is null. Is it? (No and yes, respectively — section 5.3.4.) Your compiler refuses to let you initialize a pointer-to-member-function with the address of a static member function — how come? (Because static members act like nonmembers — section 3.6.2.)

In addition to telling you what's what, the ARM provides extensive commentary on *why* many features of C++ behave the way they do. That kind of background information can make it a lot easier to swallow some of the idiosyncrasies of the language. For instance, here's something that drives most people crazy when they first encounter it:

```
class Base {
public:
  void f(int x);
};

class Derived: public Base {
public:
  void f(char *p);
};

Derived *pd = new Derived;
pd->f(10);                          // error!
```

The problem is that `Derived::f` hides `Base::f`, even though they take different parameter types, so the compiler demands that the call to f take a `char*`, which the literal 10 most certainly is not.

This is inconvenient, but the ARM provides an explanation for this behavior (section 13.1). Suppose that when you called f you really did want to call the version in Derived, but you accidentally used the wrong parameter type. Further suppose that Derived is way down in the inheritance hierarchy and that you were unaware of the fact that Derived indirectly inherits from some base class BaseClass, and that BaseClass defines a function f that takes an int. Then you would inadvertently have called BaseClass::f, a function that you didn't even know existed! This kind of error could occur frequently when large class libraries come into widespread use, so the designer of C++ decided to nip it in the bud by having derived class members shadow base class members on a per-name basis.

Note, by the way, that if the writer of class `Derived` wants to allow clients of the class to have access to `Base::f`, this is easily accomplished via a simple inline function:

```
class Derived: public Base {
public:
  void f(char *p);
  void f(int x) { Base::f(x); }
};

Derived *pd = new Derived;
pd->f(10);                         // fine
```

The ARM also gives detailed descriptions of features that are technically in the C++ language, but that currently have uneven availability in commercial compilers. The most important of these features are nested types, templates, and exceptions (see Item 49).

Index

It is an unfortunate fact of life that the term *definition* means different things in C++ and in English. In this index, the term *definition* refers to a C++ definition. English definitions — definitions of terms — are labeled "definition (English)" and are summarized under "English definitions."

Operators are listed under *operator*. That is, operator<< is listed under operator<<, not under <<, etc. The exceptions to this rule are the operators new, delete, and sizeof, which are listed, oddly enough, under new, delete, and sizeof, respectively.

The example class declarations used in this book are indexed under *example classes*. Similarly, the example functions declared and/or defined in the book are indexed under *example functions*.